MONTANA
TERRITORY
— AND THE —
CIVIL WAR

MONTANA
TERRITORY
— AND THE —
CIVIL WAR

A Frontier Forged on the Battlefield

KEN ROBISON

THE
History
PRESS

Published by The History Press
Charleston, SC 29403
www.historypress.net

Front cover: General Meagher leads the Irish Brigade at the Battle of Fair Oaks, 1862. *Courtesy of the Library of Congress, Popular Graphic Arts Collection.*

First published 2013
Second printing 2013
Third printing 2014
Fourth printing 2014

Manufactured in the United States

ISBN 978.1.62619.175.4

Library of Congress Cataloging-in-Publication Data

Robison, Ken.
Montana Territory and the Civil War : a frontier forged on the battlefield / Ken Robison.
pages cm. -- (Civil war)
ISBN 978-1-62619-175-4 (pbk.)
1. Montana--History--Civil War, 1861-1865. 2. Soldiers--Montana--Biography. 3.
Confederate States of America. Army--Officers--Biography. 4. United States. Army-
-Officers--Biography. 5. United States--History--Civil War, 1861-1865--Biography. 6.
Montana--History, Military. 7. Montana--History--19th century. I. Title.
F731.R52 2013
978.6'02--dc23
2013038884

On February 12, 1973, as Operation Homecoming began, I greeted senior navy prisoner of war (POW) Captain James Bond Stockdale on the tarmac at Clark Air Force Base in the Philippines as he flew to freedom from captivity in Hanoi. For the next two months, I had the honor of serving as his escort and debriefer as he revealed his amazing story. For his courage and leadership of our POWs in North Vietnamese prisons through harsh torture and confinement, Captain Stockdale received the Medal of Honor.

This book is dedicated to Vice Admiral James Bond Stockdale, USN, for his undaunted courage under fire.

Contents

CONTENTS

CONTENTS

Acknowledgements

My lifelong fascination with the Civil War has found satisfaction in many institutions and battlefields around the country, especially at the National Archives, Gettysburg and Virginia's research centers and many battle sites. There is simply nothing to compare with walking the hallowed grounds so important to our history.

The role of Montana Territory, its birth during the Civil War and those who came during and after the war have intrigued me. Years of researching fascinating Captain Nicholas Wall have led me all over our Big Sky country and the length of the Missouri River, always with his brief but intriguing role in the Civil War in my mind. A more recent quest has looked to other veterans—men, women and children—who lived through our nation's first "total war." Many have helped along the way.

To descendants of those who served in the Civil War who have protected and shared the diaries, letters, papers and artifacts handed down to them, my thanks and admiration, especially to Richard Thoroughman, Charles House, Jean Cobb, Neville Smith, Clint Loss, Bill Culbertson, David M. Habben, Dora Mahood, Charlene Nava and others. To those active in reenactment and veteran groups, keep up your good work. A special kudos to Michael Koury for decades of exceptional work with his Old Army Press and the Order of the Indian Wars.

Our Overholser Historical Research Center has yielded gem after gem as our volunteer staff fields the many queries that come our way. Montana Historical Society's Research Center always amazes me with its depth of treasures and willingness to help. Janet Thomson of the Great Falls Genealogy Society feeds tip after tip my way as she indexes and browses through Montana's journals and newspapers. Kay Strombo of the Mineral County Museum shares my fascination with the Civil War and over many years has compiled a list of more than 6,200 Montana Civil War veterans. Judy Ellinghausen and Kristin Bokovoy have made the impressive resources of The History Museum available. Kathy Mora and the Great Falls Public Library provide a second home filled with invaluable research resources and an inspiring place to work in the Montana Room.

A special thanks to the family of Morton I. Skari for sharing his Civil War library, and my appreciation to friend Phil Aaberg for suggesting this. To Jay Hoar, my admiration for his intrepid quest for knowledge of Civil War veterans, North and South. To Thomas and Abigail Minkler, premier collectors of Montana's historical treasures, my thanks for use of photographs.

Both the *Fort Benton River Press* and the *Great Falls Tribune* earn my appreciation for their enthusiasm to share my Civil War stories with the public throughout the sesquicentennial years. And many thanks to readers who have applauded these stories and shared their families' treasured memories.

The wonders of the Internet never cease to amaze. Online access is revolutionizing historical research—what a pleasure it is to tap the rich photographic resources of the Library of Congress; the growing collection of digital newspapers on Chronicling America; and the Civil War and family history records now online.

My appreciation to The History Press for the opportunity to contribute a Montana book for its Civil War series. From our initial conversation, my editors, Will McKay and Hilary Parrish, have been timely and talented in moving the project along. Their enthusiasm and ideas have helped immensely.

To Karin and Mark, and Mark's young boys, Perry and Turner, you are the wave of the future—my thanks and love for sharing an interest in history. And all credit to my wife, Michele, who has roamed the world with me sharing love for knowledge of the past.

Introduction

As our nation commemorates the 150th anniversary of the Civil War, it is time to ask, "How did the Civil War affect Montana?" Some might think this is a curious question since that monumental struggle began far away in "the States" before there was even a Montana Territory and ended a quarter of a century before the state of Montana entered the Union. Yet the real answer lies in the profound impact the Civil War had on our country, our people and the formation of Montana Territory. Montana became a territory forged on the battlefields of the Civil War.

The Civil War followed the secession of Southern states. From the Southern view, this was a War Between the States, a War for Southern Independence. The withdrawal of these states from the Union enabled Congress to pass momentous legislation that would forever change our future state and nation. In three short months without Southern obstructionism, Congress passed the Homestead Act, opening millions of acres of free land for western settlement; the Pacific Railway Act, paving the way for transcontinental railroads; the Morrill Land Grant College Act greatly broadening education; and legislation abolishing slavery in Washington, D.C., and the western territories. The Civil War shaped the future of Montana and the West.

In addition, the Civil War settled forever two fundamental questions—there would be a unified United States, and there would no longer be enslaved African Americans. The Civil War directly impacted every section, every community, every family and every individual. The war came at a time when the upper Missouri River region was first undergoing settlement by nonnative Americans. Gold strikes in the spring of 1862 led to the rapid formation of Montana Territory, and the extracted gold and other mineral wealth helped fill the coffers of the Federal government, directly aiding the war effort.

The Civil War accelerated the settlement and formation of Montana Territory. Its early leaders—Lincoln Republican Sidney Edgerton, War Democrat (supporting both the Union and the war) and leader of the Irish Brigade General Thomas Francis Meagher, Kentucky National Unionist Green Clay Smith and many others—came during and after the war with their lives and thoughts molded in the military and political battles of the war. Their stories sample the political framing of the new frontier territory.

The Civil War dislocated and relocated countless Americans. Some men came to the new Montana Territory to escape service or the ravages of war. Some came to "chase the elephant," seeking fortune or opportunity in the new land. Women and children followed the men arriving by steamboat or wagon into the rough Montana frontier. Shortly after the creation of Montana Territory, Governor Edgerton hastily ordered a census of the very transient mining population. That census found some 15,812 residents, with 11,493 concentrated in southwestern Madison County, mostly along the placer mining boomtowns of Alder Gulch. While home state was not recorded, many, perhaps a majority, had come from Southern and border states, very much influenced by the war.

As the war ended, more and more people came, bearing the scars and experiences of war and bringing with them their hopes, dreams and biases. They came from North and South and especially from the war-ravaged border states. Some men and women newly freed and newly citizens sought a brighter future away from the lands of their enslavement. Women found uncommon opportunity, and many took advantage of it. Men and women, black and white, came with the frontier army that moved into new military posts: Camp Cooke and Forts Shaw, Ellis, Assinniboine and the others. Many Indian Wars army men who had lived through and been affected by the Civil War continued to serve—and came to Montana Territory.

One who didn't come was Colonel Robert Gould Shaw, yet his name is still with us today. Colonel Shaw, namesake for Fort Shaw in the Sun River Valley, commanded the 54th Massachusetts Infantry, the first black regiment raised in the North. Colonel Shaw died leading his men over the breastworks at Fort Wagner on the outskirts of Charleston, South Carolina. His brave men suffered nearly 50 percent casualties, proving convincingly to both North and South that black men could fight and die every bit the equal of whites.

One of Colonel Shaw's men, Private Joseph W. Meek of the "Fighting 54th," was a freed slave who survived Fort Wagner to come to the upper Missouri in 1880 with his brother, Charles. Joe Meek mined for silver and lived for many years near White Sulphur Springs. His brother, Charles M. Meek, as a teenager served on the staff of General Ulysses Grant before joining a famed black unit, the 5th Kentucky Cavalry, U.S. Colored Troops. Charles lived in Great Falls, Montana, where he was active in Republican Party politics, and is believed to be the first black man to serve on a jury in Montana. Charles was active in the Grand Army of the Republic (GAR) until his death.

Nicholas Wall came to the upper Missouri, a paroled Confederate prisoner of war after an abortive attempt to lead Missouri into the Confederacy in May 1861. Captain Wall led the way to the gold fields for the flood of Southerners who would find refuge and opportunity away from the vicious warfare in Missouri and Tennessee.

Private Joseph O. Gregg, 133rd Ohio Infantry, received the Congressional Medal of Honor for action in June 1864 near Petersburg, Virginia. Captain Gregg came to Great Falls in 1887 and led the community in veterans' affairs. He promoted the idea of a veterans' cemetery plot and monument for Highland Cemetery and, under his leadership veterans of the GAR with Confederate veterans, designed a soldiers' monument. The group selected a plot for the monument at the entrance to the cemetery—the first in the nation dedicated jointly to both Union and Confederate soldiers.

Among the thousands of Union and Confederate veterans coming to Montana after the war, many came with the frontier army during the Indian Wars of the 1860s and '70s. Although the regular army was cut drastically in the aftermath of the Civil War, most of its leaders, both officer and enlisted, had served in the war. Thus, this postwar army brought hundreds of experienced leaders to Montana. The names of senior officers John Gibbon, O. O. Howard, George Custer and Regis de Trobriand are known to many, while junior officer Lieutenant James Bradley and enlisted Sergeant Robert Loss are not. Their stories, during the Civil War and in the postwar army, represent those who served in the frontier army.

Of the Civil War veterans who migrated to Montana Territory, this book provides a sampling of their experiences before, during and after the war. It covers the battles critical to the outcome of the war. Men, women and children came, each with their physical and mental wounds, their stories and memories. The Civil War left an indelible impression on each and every one.

In 2011, as the national commemoration of the 150th anniversary of the Civil War began, I surveyed the scene in Montana searching for insight into how this greatest conflict in our nation's history would be remembered here. I found a few articles in Montana newspapers, but after that their silence was deafening. In response, I suggested monthly articles in the *Fort Benton River Press* and the *Great Falls Tribune* to commemorate the Civil War. Both newspapers accepted my offer, and for the past two years, my articles have appeared monthly. Each story centers on a veteran or event important to Montana—where the person came from, what he did during the war, how he came to Montana Territory and what he did after settling here. Readers with Civil War ancestors who migrated to Montana were encouraged to send their family stories and photographs to mtcivilwar@yahoo.com.

The public response to my Civil War series was encouraging, and many stories were shared. Clearly, with the thousands (well over ten thousand) of veterans migrating to Montana, my series can only present a sampling, yet my goal has been to bring visibility, awareness and understanding about the Civil War to the public throughout the sesquicentennial years.

This book continues my quest to commemorate the Civil War and bring to the public knowledge of the impact of the war on Montana Territory and its people, our ancestors, during the formative years. The sampling presented here shares the stories and experiences of men, women and children from the North and the South. Among the stories are those of veterans who fought in the Eastern and Western Theaters as Rebels and Yankees, including those who survived the chaotic battlegrounds in Missouri, Tennessee, Kansas and Arkansas. Sampled are those who fought a little or a lot and those who stayed the course or cut and ran. The women who served as nurses, teachers and spies have their stories, as do the children who roamed the battlefields, forming impressions that stayed with them forever. Special tribute is paid to the black Americans who rose from slavery to freedom on the fighting fronts of their great war that extended to the postwar Reconstruction years.

As you read these stories, I hope you will gain an appreciation for the profound impact of the Civil War on our people—in Montana and throughout our nation. I hope you will join me in commemorating these veterans, Union and Confederate, and their families—they contributed more than we can ever repay.

Chapter 1

Gold Camp Rebels Versus Yankees

Dueling words rang out across the new territory of Montana in the spring of 1865. The Civil War was ending, yet harsh words and hard feelings continued to dominate the political scene. The Unionist weekly *Montana Post* of April 29, 1865, editorialized as it reported the death of President Abraham Lincoln:

> *The Dark Day. The sable borders of our columns recall to our minds the dread fact we would so willingly disbelieve, if we could; but in the sad faces of our brethren we read the unspoken query, "Know ye not that there is a prince and a great man fallen this day?" Would to God it were not so; yet alas! The black record is written on the pages of history, and the earthly tenement of as pure a soul as ever animated a mortal frame, and as noble a mind as ever planned the salvation of a people—is to-day but as a clod of the valley...*
> *"Can Honor's voice provoke the silent dust,*
> *Or flattery soothe the dull, cold ear of death?"*
> *Abraham Lincoln is basely murdered; William H. Seward, his counselor, rests on the brink of the grave. Our heart bleeds as we write; but our sorrow is not for these men, but for the people of America.*

Two weeks later, the *Post* printed a notice nailed to the door of its agent in Prickly Pear City:

Glory enough for one time!
Old Abe has gone to hell!
Hurrah for Jeff. Davis!
Grand Reception of Old Abe in Hell!
Big Dinner!
Grand Reception of Old Abe in Hell!
The Devil's Band played "Welcome the Chief!"—Notice signed "One of
the Chivalry"

To this Rebel sentiment, the *Post* responded:

We think the most ardent secessionist, out of a man-house, will consider
it time to shake his skirts clear from contact with the animated carrion
that penned this able, manly and elevating manifesto. There will ever be
some questionable forms of life, bearing the outward shape of humanity,
engendered by the festering of corruption and feeding on rottenness, like those
crawling and writhing vermin that we saw reveling on the putrid carcasses
of beasts of burden. Is this an exponent of the rank and file of secession?
We expect that Southern men will take this in hand; ferret out this brutal
defamer and punish him. One advice we give him, and that is to ask mercy
of God for his soul; for if discovered in the dunghill he may make his
home—man will have none on his body.

These were not dueling words spoken in the "occupied" South but rather in Montana Territory adjoining the North-Western Territory of Canada. Montana became a territory on May 26, 1864, just three years after the war began and just two short years after gold strikes in southwestern Montana had accelerated white settlement in this upper Missouri River region. The Gold Creek strike in the spring of 1862 was followed in rapid succession by greater discoveries at Grasshopper Creek (Bannack, 1862), Alder Gulch (1863), Last Chance Gulch (1864) and Confederate Gulch (1864). Within a year, thousands of miners, merchants and adventurers, the good and the bad, flooded into then eastern Washington Territory (1862) and later eastern Idaho Territory (1863). Gold brought the flood of miners and the very early creation of Montana Territory.

Gold and the remote geography brought large numbers of Southerners to the mining boomtowns. Those who supported the South came to seek riches or adventure, to escape war service, to honor paroles banishing them "to the western territories." As the war progressed and Confederate control

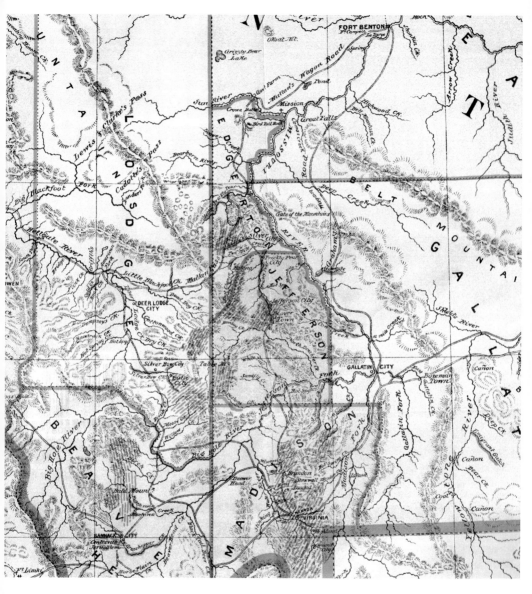

Map of Montana from Fort Benton to the gold mining camps of Bannock and Virginia City, 1865. *Author's collection.*

of Missouri and Tennessee slipped away, the flow increased, leading to Unionist belief that "the left wing of Price's Army" was flooding into the mining camps. Sterling Price, the eleventh governor of Missouri from 1853 to 1857, served as a Confederate army major general during the Civil War.

The defeat of General Price's forces in Missouri in 1864 brought a flood to the western territories. Regardless of motivation, they came with passionate beliefs—secession was good; Lincoln Republicans were bad.

THE CIVIL WAR THROUGH WORDS: VARINA VERSUS VIRGINIA CITY

As one of the new towns formed in Alder Gulch, a hotbed of Confederate sentiment, Southern sympathizers determined to name the town "Varina" in honor of the wife of Confederate president Jefferson Davis. Varina Townsite Company was formed in June 1863. Papers were drawn up using the new name and presented to miners' court Judge Dr. G. G. Bissell to finalize. The judge, an ardent Unionist, issued an emphatic expletive, declaring that he absolutely would not allow the town to be named for the first lady of the Confederacy. He boldly wrote in the name "Virginia City"; thus, that town was born, soon to be the capital of the new Territory of Montana.

The crystallization of society into a true community proved a difficult process on the frontier. In remote Montana, this process proved especially so with a population so diverse, from regions so remote from one another, with environments, entanglements and traditions so incongruous. Road agents soon followed the gold and organized around Sheriff Henry Plummer. Robberies and murders followed until a vigilante movement was organized. Meanwhile, organized government began to form around an ardent Lincoln Republican and soon-to-be first territorial governor, Sidney Edgerton.

When the first newspaper began publication in the new territory on August 27, 1864, the staunchly

Honoring Varina Davis, wife of Confederate president Jefferson Davis, triggered a raging battle in Alder Gulch in 1863. *United Confederate Veterans Convention, 1895. Author's collection.*

Mining boomtown Virginia City in 1866, later capital of Montana Territory. *Library of Congress.*

Unionist editor carried a patriotic banner on the first issue of his *Montana Post*: "My Country, May She Always Be Right, But My Country, Right or Wrong."

The stories of Nicholas Wall, James Liberty Fisk and the arrival of the military represent the early years of the Civil War in what became Montana Territory. Major Nick Wall was captured and held as a Confederate prisoner of war, banished to the western territories, joined the vigilante movement to bring law and order and established a trading empire in Territorial Montana. Captain James Fisk organized and led wagon trains from Minnesota to the upper Missouri gold fields during the Civil War to bring loyal Unionists to balance the influx of Southerners. Military presence on the upper Missouri, previously transitory, now began to man garrisons to protect white settlers from real and perceived threats from native Indians.

MONTANA'S FIRST REBEL PRISONER OF WAR AND TERRITORIAL EMPIRE BUILDER: NICHOLAS WALL[1]

Nicholas Wall was a man of many talents and important firsts in Montana history. He was the first Confederate prisoner of war to come to (later) Montana Territory. He was a founding member of the Montana Vigilantes

---

1. Earlier version published in *Fort Benton River Press* (hereafter *River Press*), June 26, 2013.

and among the most important businessmen of Montana Territory, yet few Montanans have ever heard of Captain Nicholas Wall.

Nicholas Wall was born in Alexandria, Virginia, in 1820. He was a young steamboat captain on the Mississippi River in the 1840s and operated a steamboat agency in St. Louis a decade later. Wall lived with his family in St. Louis, where they had one female domestic slave in the household in 1860. Major Nick Wall was officer of commissary with the Missouri Volunteer Militia when it deployed to the southwestern Missouri border with Kansas in late November 1860 to suppress raids by Kansas Jayhawkers on the eve of the Civil War. As commissary of the brigade on this Southwest Expedition, Major Wall made all purchases and issued all rations and stores. The brigade returned to St. Louis in mid-December to be welcomed home by immense crowds.

By early May 1861, Missouri teetered on the edge of secession. Missouri's pro-secession governor Claiborne Jackson, supported by Brigadier General Daniel M. Frost, commanding the Missouri Militia, and the Southern-leaning officers on his staff, including Major Wall, were determined to lead the state out of the Union. The Civil War began in Missouri on May 6, 1861, when the Missouri Militia was ordered into encampment at Camp Jackson at Lindell's Grove on the outskirts of St. Louis. Camp Jackson posed a symbolic and potentially real threat to the Union in Missouri. In response, Captain Nathaniel Lyon led loyal Union troops composed mostly of German immigrants to surround Camp Jackson. In the face of overwhelming firepower, the Missouri Militia surrendered without firing a shot, and its secession flags were hauled down.

Major Wall and the other officers and men of the Missouri Militia were held as Confederate prisoners of war and marched through the streets to the St. Louis Arsenal. During the march, riots and gunfire broke out and continued for two days. The prisoners were released on parole that required them either to remain in St. Louis or go to the western territories.

After signing his parole, Nick Wall's Civil War was over. During July 1861, he commanded the steamboat *Emilie* in place of Captain Joe LaBarge, who, ironically, was removed from his command because of his pro-Southern leanings. In the spring of 1862, the *Emilie*, with Captain LaBarge back in command and Captain Wall serving as clerk, departed St. Louis loaded with 143 miners and adventurers bound for the gold fields of Idaho. Steamboat clerks were responsible for handling cargo and passengers.

The *Emilie* landed at Fort Benton on June 17, 1862, and Captain Nick Wall stepped ashore in what would become Montana Territory to establish the most sophisticated trading empire of the 1860s. With the miners, Wall headed west along the newly completed Mullan Road to western Montana, where gold had been discovered in quantities at Gold Creek near today's Drummond. Arriving in the new mining area, Wall leased cabins from Johnny Grant and set up a small store, doing a brisk business with newly arriving miners.

Just weeks later, Wall had a visitor at his store. Young Tom Cover arrived with a group of men who were out of money and starving. Looking Cover over, Wall advanced him lifesaving provisions, and before long, Cover, with another party, discovered gold at Grasshopper Creek, the beginning of the Bannack boom. In payment, Cover filed a claim in Nick Wall's name. Wall moved his store to Bannack and early on became a partner in the Bannack Ditch that furnished water to the placer miners.

After a successful trading year, Nick Wall returned overland to St. Louis for the winter, establishing a commuter pattern he would follow throughout his Montana years. During the winter of 1862–63, Wall formed a partnership with St. Louis steamboat owner and merchant John J. Roe, who was acquiring wealth from pork packing during the Civil War.

On his return to the mountains in early June 1863, Captain Wall rode into Bannack and then on to Fort Benton to receive a large shipment for the newly formed John J. Roe & Company. This freight had been shipped up the Missouri River by Captain Joe LaBarge's steamboat *Shreveport*, commanded by his brother John LaBarge. Through a combination of low water and bad judgment, *Shreveport*'s freight was offloaded at Snake Point, an inaccessible location on the river. Disgusted at this setback to his new company, Captain Wall immediately sent a letter of protest and returned to St. Louis to join John J. Roe in seeking damages in district court from LaBarge, Harkness & Company. In mid-September, accompanied by young Edgar G. Maclay, Captain Wall returned to Bannack, and on November 1, Wall and Maclay arrived in the new boomtown of Virginia City in the heart of Alder Gulch's massive placer mines. Captain Wall opened the John J. Roe & Company store and erected a pretentious-looking house in the rear. True to his nautical life, his home resembled a "Texas," or captain's cabin on the upper deck of a steamboat.

With the mining boom of the big gold strikes at Grasshopper Creek and Alder Gulch, thousands of miners, merchants and adventurers flocked into this eastern region of the new Idaho Territory. In the presence of huge amounts of gold and in the absence of civil authority or organized government, travelers were increasingly subjected to robbery and murder. "Miners' courts" tried to fill the void, and by mid-December, one of the murderers, George Ives, was apprehended and brought to trial in Virginia City.

A young Civil War Union veteran, Colonel Wilbur Fisk Sanders of Bannack, accepted the dangerous challenge of prosecuting Ives, who was known to be an associate of Sheriff Henry Plummer, leader of the gang of troublemakers. Despite threats to his life, Sanders began to prosecute. Throughout the Ives trial, Colonel Sanders was a guest of Captain Wall, and Wall's men served as guards at the trial and at his home. Early in the Ives trial, probably on the night of December 20, 1863, Wall met covertly in the back of Kinna & Nye's store with four fellow Masons: Paris S. Pfouts, Alvin W. Brookie, John Nye and Wilbur F. Sanders. Masonic bonds trumped North-South sentiment, and out of this meeting came agreement to form a vigilante movement to bring order out of the lawless chaos. After Ives's conviction and hanging, Captain Wall departed Virginia City by horseback for St. Louis. His arrival at Salt Lake City on January 12, 1864, brought the first news to the outside world of the vigilante actions to clean up the gold fields.

During this winter sojourn in St. Louis, Captain Wall and John J. Roe developed the next step in their plan. By the spring of 1864, their new steamboat line, the Montana and Idaho Transportation Company, had begun operations under Roe's son-in-law, Captain John G. Copelin. By late April, Captain Wall was back in Montana Territory just as it was being formed, taking charge of Roe company operations. During this summer, E.G. Maclay suggested that they begin an overland freighting operation, thus perfecting their network: shipping cargo up the Missouri River on company boats; freighting the cargo overland by company wagon trains; and selling the merchandise in John J. Roe & Company stores. Over the coming years, Captain Wall built the overland freighting operation, forming the famed Diamond R freighting line—the "R" a tribute to their St. Louis financier, John J. Roe.

As his workforce of men grew, Captain Wall attained the capability to raise a small volunteer armed force at Fort Benton to react to increasing incidents in 1865 with Blackfoot renegades such as the Ophir massacre on the Marias River in May by Calf Shirt's band. The Montana Militia, formed by Acting Governor Thomas Francis Meagher, and the beginning of a U.S. Army presence soon replaced Captain Wall's volunteer force.

Wall continued to build the powerful John J. Roe & Company operations in Montana. As Last Chance Gulch boomed in 1864 and the town of Helena grew, Wall moved his company's headquarters to Helena. Throughout Wall's tenure in Montana Territory, he was known and respected and the company prospered, but he remained quietly out of politics. In June 1868, as the Montana placer mines began to fade, Captain Wall arranged the sale of

Nicholas Wall Family Mausoleum in Bellefontaine Cemetery, St. Louis. *David M. Habben Collection.*

the great John J. Roe & Company's Diamond R to E.G. Maclay & Company, a group that included men working for the company.

Despite his company's withdrawal, Captain Wall continued to spend summers in Montana Territory, looking after his interests in the Bannack Ditch and mining properties. Mainly, the popular Nicholas Wall, the first Confederate Civil War prisoner of war to come to the upper Missouri, visited the towns and friends he had made in his wartime exile years. On October 2, 1880, Captain Nicholas Wall passed away in St. Louis and was interred in an exceptional mausoleum at Bellefontaine Cemetery.

HO! FOR THE GOLD FIELDS: THE FISK FAMILY IN WAR AND IN PEACE

The importance to the Union of new loyal territories and Montana gold and the need to balance Confederate influence in the upper Missouri region led the Federal government to encourage and support emigration from Minnesota westward to the gold fields. Between 1862 and 1867, eight wagon trains traveled the Northern Overland Wagon Road via Fort Benton to the Montana gold fields, bringing perhaps 1,400 settlers mostly from the northern tier of states. Most expeditions organized into companies, while some had military escorts.

James Liberty Fisk was born in New York of Irish heritage, one of six boys who would play an enormous role in Montana history. Early in life he moved to Minnesota and became fascinated by the western frontier. In October 1861, Fisk enlisted as a private in Company B, 3rd Minnesota Infantry Regiment. The following year, he was promoted to captain and called to Washington, D.C., for appointment as superintendent of emigration of a route between Fort Abercrombie and Fort Walla Walla, Washington Territory. Captain Fisk was assigned to the U.S. Volunteers Quartermaster's Department Infantry Regiment and operated independently on detached duty directly under the secretary of war.

Returning to Minnesota, Captain Fisk quickly organized his first expedition of 130 men and women with fifty-three wagons. Traveling the Northern Overland Route used by Governor Isaac I. Stevens on his Pacific Railway Survey expedition in 1853, the first Fisk expedition arrived at Fort Benton on September 5, 1862. Over the next several years, Captain Fisk led three more expeditions, and four other parties brought wagon trains to the Montana mining frontier.

James Fisk and four of his brothers served in the Civil War, and all six eventually became residents of Montana Territory. At the close of the war, after four years and four months of service, Captain James Fisk was mustered out. He at once prepared for another overland trip, and in the summer of 1866—in company with his war veteran brothers, Robert E., Van H. and Andrew J.—he migrated to Montana, arriving in Helena in August. This last Fisk Expedition was the largest, with five hundred settlers in 160 wagons.

Robert E. Fisk was born in Pierpont, Ohio, in 1837. He spent his early life as a newspaperman in Indiana and New York before the Civil War. In June 1862, he was commissioned first lieutenant in Company I, 53rd New York Infantry. Four months later, he transferred to Company G, 132nd New York Infantry Regiment. Promoted to captain in March 1863, he mustered out in June 1865 at Salisbury, North Carolina. During the war, Captain Fisk corresponded with Miss Elizabeth "Lizzie" Chester of Vernon, Connecticut, and she later became his wife. He served as second-in-command during the 1866 Fisk Expedition and arrived in Helena in September of that year. The following November, the *Helena Herald* began operations from the top floor of a two-story log building. For thirty-six years, helped by his brothers,

Ho! For the Gold Fields: Fisk Northern Overland Wagon Trains, 1866. *Author's collection.*

Robert E. Fisk owned and edited the *Helena Herald*, actively promoting the Republican cause in Montana.

Van Hayden Fisk enlisted as a private in Company I, 1st Minnesota Infantry in September 1861 and was discharged for disability eighteen months later. Andrew Jackson Fisk enlisted at age eighteen in Company A, 2nd Minnesota Cavalry, in October 1863 and served until discharged in April 1866, just in time to join the 1866 expedition. Daniel Willard Fisk enlisted in Company I, 7th Minnesota Infantry, in August 1862 and served for three years.

The Fisk brothers' involvement in Montana politics and their accomplishments in private enterprise together with their work as guides made the Fisks one of Montana's more historically notable families. In addition, through her extensive letters to her family in the East, Lizzie Fisk documented daily life and the story of early frontier Montana in an exceptional way.

ARMING MONTANA:
ARRIVAL OF THE MILITARY ON THE UPPER MISSOURI

The Lewis and Clark Corps of Discovery in 1805–06 brought the first American soldiers to the upper Missouri region. In the following decades, occasional veterans like Malcolm Clarke (Mexican War) came to the region to join in the fur trade or for adventure. In 1853–54, the Isaac I. Stevens Pacific Railway Survey was escorted by an army detachment that included First Lieutenant John Mullan. It was not until the remarkable summer of 1860 that a large army contingent arrived in the area. Throughout the spring and summer of 1860, First Lieutenant John Mullan, a topographical engineer, led a combined military and civilian workforce building a military wagon road from western Montana and arriving at Fort Benton on August 1.

One month earlier, the *Chippewa* and *Key West* became the first steamboats to arrive at the Fort Benton levee. Onboard were some three hundred U.S. Army First Dragoons under Major George A.H. Blake, arriving to become the first military users upon completion of the 624-mile Mullan Military Wagon Road from Fort Benton to Fort Walla Walla, Washington Territory. Also arriving at Fort Benton in July was the U.S. Army Raynolds Expedition after extensive explorations of the Yellowstone and Missouri Rivers.

With the Mullan Expedition in 1860 was a military escort of some 140 men from the 3rd Artillery Regiment, including quartermaster civilian wagoneers. Two of the officers, Lieutenant Harlan Benton Lyon and Lieutenant James Lyon White, had been Military Academy classmates of Mullan's. In 1861, both resigned their commissions to join the Army of the Confederacy. For two more years, Captain Mullan continued construction of the wagon road before resigning from the army in 1863.

Discovery of gold in southwestern Montana in 1862 changed the complexion of the steamboat trade as it evolved from support for the fur trade and Indian annuities to become a major highway to the gold fields. The intense fighting and guerrilla warfare in Missouri and Kansas and the Sioux wars in the Dakotas during the early years of the Civil War disrupted steamboat operations, and it wasn't until 1864 that St. Louis merchants began to realize the immense profits to be made from the "mountain" trade. In addition to the large-scale passenger and freight traffic coming upriver by steamboat, bison robes and gold were shipped down. Historian Joel F. Overholser estimated that five-sixths of the gold from Montana mines, about $90 million between 1862 and 1866, went down the Missouri River, mostly to St. Louis safely under Union control. The steamboat *Luella* alone carried two and a half tons of gold dust, worth $1,250,000, down the Missouri on a single trip in 1866.

Overland routes via St. Joseph and Salt Lake City also brought many settlers to the new Montana Territory. With the increased flow of miners and settlers, pressure on native Indians increased, and incidents along Montana's Benton Road, the Bozeman Trail and other trails became frequent occurrences. Incidents targeting steamers along the important Missouri River corridor in the Dakota and eastern Montana Territory increased.

Small private civilian armies and a fledgling Montana Militia tried to fill the void but proved inadequate. Calls for a permanent army presence in the new territory led to arms shipments, but few troops were available to respond until after the war.

The first soldiers to be stationed in Montana at Fort Benton, though only briefly, were, oddly, ex-Confederate soldiers called "Galvanized Yankees." These were Confederates captured by Union forces who chose to enlist for frontier service rather than remain in prisoner of war camps. On May 12, 1865, First Lieutenant Horace S. Hutchins of Company H, 1st U.S. Volunteers, and nine men embarked the steamboat *Deer Lodge* at Fort Rice, Dakota Territory, under orders from their commander, Colonel Charles Dimon, "to control the trade with Indians between [Fort Benton] and Fort Union." The *Deer Lodge* arrived at Fort Benton on May 30, and the soldiers remained during the summer to provide transportation security.

Five days prior to the army's arrival at Fort Benton, ten woodcutters nearby were killed by Kainai Blackfoot led by war chief Calf Shirt. This and other incidents led Acting Governor Thomas Francis Meagher to raise a militia company and call for troops and arms from the Federal government.

The first steamboat arrival of 1865 at Fort Benton was the American Fur Company's steamer *Yellowstone* on May 28, but not without adventure. The boat had been refitted and lengthened and the draught lightened, and it left St. Louis on March 20. Historian Joel Overholser described the tension as the Civil War neared its end:

> *Charles Chouteau and the new owners of the trading post at Fort Benton [Hubbell and Hawley] were aboard. There was the almost routine sniping by hostile Sioux. At old Fort Sully (present Pierre) passengers heard the news of Lincoln's assassination, and when the* Yellowstone *reached Fort Rice, Col. Charles Dimon met the boat and placed the whole party under arrest for "jubilating over" Lincoln's death. Dimon then threatened to have Chouteau shot for his assumed Confederate sympathies. Although*

Steamboats at the Fort Benton levee in 1867. *Overholser Historical Research Center.*

actions of the company during the Civil War provided no positive evidence of such, the suspicions probably influenced revocation of the Chouteau company's license for Indian trading. Intervention by Northerners Hubbell and Hawley resulted in Dimon's giving up on his firing squad. As Dimon's command was of ex-Confederate soldiers…one might wonder about their willingness to carry out any firing squad service.

Chapter 2

Montana Territory

Forged on the Battlefield

A nxious to admit free territories to the Union and helped along with personal lobbying by Sidney Edgerton, a friend and chief justice of Idaho Territory, on May 26, 1864, President Abraham Lincoln signed "An Act to provide a temporary Government for the Territory of Montana." The Civil War was at a critical stage, with General Ulysses Grant applying near-continuous pressure on General Robert E. Lee in a series of bloody battles in central Virginia that began at the Wilderness, extended to Spotsylvania and was just underway at Cold Harbor. The terrible fighting and heavy losses in Virginia weighed heavily on public opinion.

The convention to re-nominate President Lincoln was to meet at Baltimore in just twelve days' time in the second week of June 1864. To attract the support of as many War Democrats as possible, the Republican convention of 1864 was named the Union National Convention. As a new territory, Montana was entitled to one delegate at that convention. Judge Edgerton, an Ohioan and ardent antislavery Republican; Samuel T. Hauser, a War Democrat who arrived at Fort Benton on the steamboat *Emilie* in 1862; and Nathaniel Langford, another War Democrat who came west with the 1862 Fisk Expedition, all were in Washington at this time. The three "Montanans" met, passed resolutions supporting the Union and elected Langford delegate to represent the new territory at Baltimore. Langford was admitted to the Union National Convention and voted for Lincoln's re-nomination.

Later in the month, on June 22, President Lincoln appointed Sidney Edgerton governor of Montana Territory, and Edgerton became the first of a series of Civil War veterans to serve as territorial governor. Thomas Francis Meagher, a larger-than-life Irish national hero and Civil War commander of the Irish Brigade, followed Governor Edgerton. Next came Green Clay Smith from Kentucky, a War Democrat who had narrowly lost the 1864 vice presidential nomination to fellow Kentuckian Andrew Johnson. James M. Ashley, who led congressional passage of the Organic Act creating Montana Territory, came to govern the new territory, failed and left shortly after.

Montana Territory was forged on the battlefield and led by combat veterans of the Civil War. Two war veterans among all others led their respective parties during the territorial years. Major Martin Maginnis, a hero at Gettysburg and a War Democrat, led the Democrats to victory after victory as a popular delegate representing Montana Territory in Congress. Wilbur Fisk Sanders, nephew of Governor Edgerton and a staunch Lincoln Republican, led Republicans through years of narrow defeat to become one of Montana's U.S. senators when Montana was admitted to the Union in 1889.

MONTANA TERRITORIAL GOVERNORS SERVED IN THE CIVIL WAR: DEMOCRAT AND REPUBLICAN

For the first two decades, all Montana territorial governors served in the military during the Civil War except Governor James M. Ashley, who played a vital role in Congress throughout the war, and Acting Governor James Tufts, who served in government in the western territories of Dakota and Idaho during the war. All six other governors of territorial Montana fought for the Union.

First Governor Sidney Edgerton served as an abolitionist Republican congressman from Akron, Ohio, when the Civil War began. Before leaving Congress in 1862, Edgerton was appointed colonel in the Ohio Squirrel Hunters, militia volunteers who were expert shots and assigned to defend Cincinnati when Confederate brigadier general Henry Heth threatened it in the fall of 1862. The next spring, President Lincoln appointed Edgerton to be chief justice of the new Idaho Territory. Traveling overland, the Edgerton family—accompanied by niece Lucia Darling, nephew Colonel Wilbur Fisk Sanders and his family and two family friends—arrived at Bannack on September 16, 1863. Bannack was booming with placer gold mining, and Edgerton quickly realized the value

Montana's first territorial governor, Sidney Edgerton.
Thomas Minkler Collection.

of the gold fields at Bannack and Alder Gulch to the Union in funding the war and developing a territory. Edgerton, accompanied by Sanders, traveled to Washington, D.C., to lobby for creation of a territory separated from Idaho. His lobbying succeeded, and in 1864, Montana was created from Idaho and Dakota Territories. On June 22, 1864, President Lincoln appointed Sidney Edgerton governor of the new territory, with Bannack as capital.

During Edgerton's absence, in December 1863 and January 1864, Wilbur F. Sanders helped form a covert vigilante group to restore law and order from corrupt Sheriff Henry Plummer and his allies, who had been robbing and terrorizing traveling miners. Upon Edgerton's return, a census was hurriedly held, followed by elections to organize the territorial government. When the first territorial legislature convened in December 1864, Governor Edgerton insisted that each legislator sign a loyalty oath. John H. Rogers, elected to the House of Representatives from Madison County, refused to sign the oath— he had fought for the Confederacy as a lieutenant under General Sterling Price in Missouri. In the words of Joseph Kinsey Howard, in Rogers's "little gesture the Confederacy fought a last battle for the western Territories, and lost." After battling the legislature, in September 1865, Governor Edgerton again departed Montana Territory, determined to convince Congress to increase funding for the new territory.

In the absence of the governor, territorial secretary Thomas Francis Meagher became acting governor. The colorful, eloquent hero of the Irish Brigade in the Civil War, Meagher had a stormy reign in Montana Territory that ended in mystery. At the beginning of the Civil War, Meagher, an Irish revolutionary and exile, although a Democrat supported the Union and campaigned vigorously to convince his fellow Irishmen to join the Union army. He raised Company K, 69th New York Infantry, the famed "Fighting 69th." Meagher

General Thomas Francis Meagher commanding the Irish Brigade in the Civil War. *Author's collection.*

soon formed the Irish Brigade and was commissioned brigadier general. Under Meagher's leadership, the Irish Brigade acquired a reputation for bravery and fighting effectiveness at Antietam, Fredericksburg and other battles suffering horrific casualties. Meagher resigned from the army on May 15, 1865, and was appointed secretary of Montana Territory by President Andrew Johnson.

Just months after Meagher's arrival at Bannack, Governor Edgerton departed for Washington, and Meagher became acting governor. Popular with many residents and the Democratic legislative branch, Meagher had a rocky relationship with the Republican executive and judicial branches and the most prominent newspaper, the *Montana Post.* In addition, the Democrats were split between War Democrats and the many Peace Democrats and the large numbers of former Confederate soldiers and sympathizers who flooded into the western territories during the war. War Democrats supported the Union and the war effort, while Peace Democrats favored a negotiated peace with the South. Meagher called the second legislature into session, although it was later ruled illegal. Meagher's first tenure extended until October 1866, ending with the arrival of new Governor Green Clay Smith, a War Democrat and Unionist from Kentucky.

In December 1866, Meagher became acting governor for a second time when Governor Smith left the territory to bring his family up the Missouri River. During early 1867, incidents between white settlers and renegades from several Blackfoot bands increased, causing Acting Governor Meagher to raise a militia. With a military escort, Meagher started to Fort Benton to meet expected Federal arms shipments. On June 23, before reaching Sun River Crossing, Meagher met returning Governor Smith and relinquished the governorship. Meagher arrived at Fort Benton on July 1 and drowned mysteriously in the Missouri River.

Green Clay Smith served as lieutenant in Company H, 1st Kentucky Cavalry, in the Mexican War. In April 1862, he assumed command, as colonel, of the 4th Kentucky Cavalry. The following month, he was severely wounded in an engagement against John H. Morgan's Confederate cavalry. Promoted to brigadier general, Smith assumed command of a cavalry brigade. He was elected to Congress and served from 1863 to 1867. During the Republican convention in 1864, Smith lost the

Green Clay Smith, loyal Unionist from Kentucky and governor of Territorial Montana. *Library of Congress.*

nomination for vice president by a single vote to Andrew Johnson. Governor Smith served as territorial governor from July 1866 to January 1867 and from July 1867 to April 1869, when he resigned to return to Kentucky.

James Tufts, a Republican from New Hampshire, replaced Meagher as secretary of the territory in March 1867 and served two years. Tufts spent the duration of the Civil War in Dakota and Idaho Territories, serving in the Idaho legislature. In Montana, Tufts served as acting governor until the arrival of Ashley in the summer of 1869.

James M. Ashley served in Congress throughout the Civil War as a Radical Republican and staunch abolitionist from Ohio. In Congress, he played a key role in the formation of Montana Territory and in passage of the antislavery Thirteenth Amendment to the Constitution. Appointed by President Grant, Ashley arrived in Montana with a reputation and an attitude. For leading the impeachment fight against Andrew Johnson, he was ridiculed as "Ashley the Impeacher." His tenure as governor was stormy and brief, as he faced a powerful Democratic majority in the territorial legislature.

Ashley's successor was fellow Republican Benjamin F. Potts, a protégé of General William T. Sherman. Formerly a Democrat, Potts switched his allegiance to the Republican Party at the beginning of the war. He immediately joined the 32nd Ohio Infantry and was elected captain. Serving throughout the war, Potts was captured at the Battle of Harpers Ferry and later paroled. Potts advanced in rank to brigadier general, commanding a brigade, and participated in the Siege of Vicksburg and the Atlanta Campaign. His confirmation as governor proved a slow process in the Senate, but he finally arrived in Virginia City at the end of August 1870.

Wiley Scribner, a Republican and veteran of the 16th Wisconsin Infantry, served as acting governor from December 1869 to August 1870, when Potts arrived.

Governor Potts skillfully brought bipartisan stability to calm the previous chaotic Montana political environment. Politics continued but at a more civil temperature, and although he remained a Republican, he cooperated remarkably well with the Democrats. Minnesota war hero Martin Maginnis served as delegate in Washington for most of Potts's years, and the two cooperated to the benefit of the territory. Governor Potts served a long tenure as governor until January 1883.

The last Civil War veteran to serve as territorial governor, John Schuyler Crosby, was appointed by President Chester Arthur. Crosby, a New Yorker, was a veteran of both the Civil War and the Indian campaigns with General Phil Sheridan. During the Civil War, Crosby served as lieutenant in the 1st U.S. Artillery. Later in the war, he became assistant inspector general under General Sheridan and remained on Sheridan's staff during the Indian Wars as a brevet lieutenant colonel aide-de-camp and adjutant general.

A more conservative Republican than Potts, Governor Crosby served until December 15, 1884. None of his successors—Republican Benjamin Platt Carpenter, Samuel Hauser and Preston Leslie (both Democrats) or the last territorial governor, Benjamin F. White (Republican)—served in the war. Time was marching on.

THE LEGEND AND MYSTERY:
GENERAL THOMAS FRANCIS MEAGHER[2]

Born in strife, lived a life of legend, died in mystery. No more fitting epitaph could be written for the larger-than-life Thomas Francis Meagher. Exiled Irish patriot, heroic Civil War leader of the Irish Brigade, colorful speaker and writer, controversial acting governor of Montana Territory—each step of his life brought fame and controversy.

---

2. Earlier version published in *River Press*, June 26, 2009.

At midday on July 1, 1867, General Thomas Francis Meagher rode hard with a militia escort along Montana's Benton Road, down the opening from the bluffs overlooking wild and wooly Fort Benton, and entered the pages of history and the stuff of legends. Ten hours later, the former acting governor of Montana Territory was dead—his death shrouded in mystery and his body lost to the depths, swift current and killer undertow of the spring rise in the Missouri River.

After recovering from war wounds suffered at the Battle of Fredericksburg, General Meagher came to frontier Montana as territorial secretary and became acting governor upon the departure of Governor Sidney Edgerton in 1865. The brilliant but brash and unpredictable Meagher, with his wife, Elizabeth, was the center of the social and political scene of the new territory during the booming gold mining days. Revered in Fenian Irish and democratic circles, Governor Meagher fought political battles with the strong Lincoln Republican element. The arrival of Governor Smith in the fall of 1866 relieved Meagher of many of his demanding duties as governor. However, Smith left the territory in early 1867, and Meagher again became acting governor. By the spring of 1867, Montana Territory faced an expanding settler population and a perceived threat from native Indians. Ever hard charging, Meagher called for Federal troops, only to be answered by a shipment of arms to the new army post Camp Cooke on the Missouri at the mouth of the Judith River. Meagher determined to go to Fort Benton to receive the arms there or embark a steamboat to go down to Camp Cooke.

Meagher departed Virginia City about June 17, accompanied by an escort of about six militiamen. He arrived in Helena on June 19, spent several days and left in ill health for Fort Benton about June 22. The next day on the Benton Road, Meagher met returning Governor Green Clay Smith and his family, who had arrived at Fort Benton on June 20 on the steamboat *Octavia*. With their brief meeting, General Meagher relinquished the governorship.

By the evening of June 23, General Meagher had arrived at John J. Healy's trading post at Sun River Crossing. On the road from Helena, Meagher suffered from severe dysentery. In the words of Meagher biographer Paul Wylie, "Years of drinking and the rigors of his chaotic life had taken their toll." For the next week, Meagher remained at Healy's post recovering from his illness. A week with colorful Irishmen Johnny Healy and Meagher, no doubt drinking and swapping tales, must have been something to behold. On the evening of June 30, a blacksmith working for Huntley Stage Line enjoyed an evening dinner "laughing and joking" with General Meagher's party at Healy's post.

Early the next morning, General Meagher and escort departed Sun River Crossing for Benton, arriving tired and dusty around noon on July 1. The view they saw from the bluffs overlooking Fort Benton is today hard to imagine. At the Fort Benton levee that day were four steamboats, all sternwheelers: the *Amaranth*, *G.A. Thomson*, *Gallatin* and *Guidon*. The *G.A. Thomson*, under Captain J.M. Woods, Clerk J. Stewart and pilot John T. Doran, had landed the previous day, completing a hard sixty-seven-day trip from St. Louis, suffering damage to the upper deck railing from a collision en route. The steamer *Gallatin* had arrived at the levee earlier on the morning of July 1 with a load of government freight from Camp Cooke but no arms. The *Guidon*, serving throughout the boating season as tender on the upper Missouri, had arrived on June 20 with 57 passengers plus an additional 130 passengers from Camp Cooke who had been stranded by the earlier sinking of the steamboat *Nora*. The *Guidon* was moored astern the *G.A. Thomson* at the Fort Benton levee.

During the year 1867, some forty-one steamboats departed St. Louis and, after the 2,400-mile trip through snags, rocks and sandbars, arrived at the Fort Benton levee between May 25 and August 8. These massive boats, each 150 to 250 feet in length, carried about two hundred tons of freight each, bringing a total of more than eight thousand tons to the Fort Benton levee.

Some eight hundred tons of freight had arrived on the levee during the past week. Part of this massive cargo had been loaded and was already moving along the Benton Road, but several hundred tons more remained on the levee. Many wagons and men, hundreds of oxen, mules and horses were loading and moving from the levee through the streets of Fort Benton and onto the trails leading in every direction from Fort Benton. From four to eight yoke of oxen drew each wagon, carrying about two or three tons of freight.

Frontier Fort Benton was earning a reputation as the "Bloodiest Block in the West," and in the summer of 1867, businesses like Mose Solomon's Medicine Lodge and the Jungle were roaring day and night. It was from the second story of the Jungle's flimsy frame earlier in June that infamous Eleanor Dumont, known as Madame Mustache, had left her blackjack game, sprinted across the street to the levee, flourished two pistols and warned off the steamer *Walter B. Dance*, reported to have smallpox aboard.

Adding to this wild and wooly environment, tensions had risen with native Indians in recent months, reports had come of the latest failed Fenian invasion of the British Possessions the previous year and territorial political and social antagonisms had increased. As General Meagher rode into town, weighing heavily on his mind no doubt was the fact that he was in debt, out of work and the subject of immense controversy, beloved by some, hated by others.

Republican leader and political adversary Wilbur Fisk Sanders was present in Fort Benton at the time, awaiting the arrival of his family on the steamboat *Abeona*. Sanders greeted General Meagher and spent part of the early afternoon with him. Fort Benton merchant I.G. Baker met Meagher on the levee and invited him to dinner at his house. During their conversation, Meagher announced that he was going downriver to receive an arms shipment.

Meagher spent much of the afternoon in the back room of Baker's store, where he read, greeted visitors and wrote correspondence. It was there that Meagher wrote his last letter, imploring territorial auditor Ming to pay back wages to ease his serious financial woes.

After spending the afternoon at the Baker store and eating supper at Baker's house, Meagher boarded the steamboat *G.A. Thomson* to spend the night. He was never seen again, and his body was never found. Did he die from Masonic vengeance? Trip and fall from the weakened railing on the upper deck of the steamboat? Jump in frustration over failed finances? That is the great mystery of General Meagher's death in Fort Benton and the birth of a legend.

Historian Paul R. Wylie's *The Irish General Thomas Francis Meagher* carefully sorts through the conflicting accounts of the general's last day. Wylie explores the accounts of Wilbur Fisk Sanders, I.G. Baker, pilot Johnny Doran and others and examines possible suspects including the vigilantes, anti-Irish hotheads, enemies such as Indian agents Augustus Chapman and Major George B. Wright. These accounts, conflicting often in detail and tone, make fascinating reading as Wylie also weighs the evidence for an act of suicide or a tragic accident to explain the death.

Weighing the evidence, this writer has reached the following conclusion. In the afternoon of July 1, General Meagher was sober but still suffering from dysentery. During the afternoon, I.G. Baker offered Meagher several glasses of blackberry wine, commonly used then to cure diarrhea. Accounts vary about where Meagher dined that evening, either with Pilot Johnny Doran on board the *G.A. Thomson* or at Baker's home. Most likely, Meagher ate at Baker's home, leaving by 7:00 p.m. Toward dusk, Meagher sat with a group of men in front of Baker's store. The party got loud, and Meagher began exhibiting possible symptoms of delusion, expressing concern that his enemies were about to do him harm. Doran got Meagher onboard the *G.A. Thomson*. There, Meagher, Doran, James M. Woods (captain of the boat) and others began drinking in the boat's salon, and Meagher became inebriated. Doran eventually got Meagher into the cabin of Captain Woods, the outside door of which faced the water. Meagher got ready for bed, and Doran left him thinking his friend was asleep and proceeded to the lower deck.

About 10:00 p.m., Doran heard a splash in the water and heard the cry "man overboard," likely uttered by the boat's black American barber who was on watch and had caught a glimpse of a man in the water. Most likely General Meagher, dressed in his underclothes, suffering from exhaustion and too much to drink and weakened by his severe bout of diarrhea, opened the cabin door to go onto the upper deck to relieve himself at the stern of the boat. There he stumbled and fell overboard from a portion of the deck that had been damaged by the earlier collision, with part of the deck railing broken off.

At least four witnesses saw Meagher fall from the boat. One credible witness, Ferdinand Roosevelt, then Wells Fargo agent at Fort Benton, saw Meagher fall overboard and testified that there was no attacker and that Meagher had been drinking heavily. Pilot Doran described the waters as "instant death—water twelve feet deep and rushing at the rate of ten miles an hour." Floating lifebuoys were put out, lights were lit, a boat was launched and every exertion was made to locate and recover the body. The search continued for several days before it was called off. It would not be the first drowning victim never found in "the big Muddy." General Thomas Francis Meagher's body was lost to the ages, but his spirit lived on.

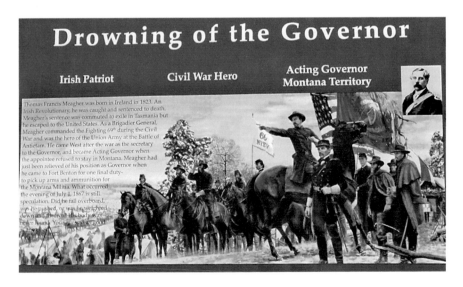

Tribute sign "Drowning of the Governor" on the Fort Benton Levee. *Author's collection.*

Upon hearing the news, Governor Smith issued a proclamation ordering tributes of respect and offering a reward for recovery of Meagher's body. Flags of Meagher's native Ireland and his adopted country were flown at half-mast as a mark of respect to his memory. A large citizens' meeting was held in Helena to mourn the general's death, with speakers proclaiming, "Our country has lost a true patriot, a friend of universal liberty, a sympathizer with the afflicted of all nations, a foe to tyranny, a fearless and intrepid general, a man of genius and of eloquence, who, at all times was ready to sacrifice personal interest for the public good."

Fort Benton returned to normalcy quickly, with steamboats coming and going with regularity. The *G.A. Thomson* left for St. Louis at noon on July 2 with about twenty passengers, "the majority of whom were returning pilgrims, disgusted with the country." Fort Benton celebrated July 4, firing off all cannons in town. At two o'clock on board the steamer *Antelope*, a large audience assembled to listen to an Independence Day oration by Colonel Sanders. In the evening, the celebration was closed by a dance, well attended by most of the community of robe traders, native Indian wives, bullwhackers and pilgrims. Innumerable fights did not disrupt the good times for most. By then, the search for General Meagher's body had been abandoned.

The steamer *Gallatin* arrived that evening, landing a battery of 6 twelve-pound mountain howitzers, 2,500 muskets and an immense amount of ammunition for the use of the Montana Militia. General Meagher's arms had arrived, but he was not there to meet them.

On June 26–28, 2009, 142 years later, Fort Benton held its annual Summer Celebration with the theme "With an Irish Flair" in honor of Montana's acting governor, Thomas Francis Meagher. The weekend events featured Paul Wylie's play *A Coroner's Inquest into the Death of Thomas Francis Meagher*; Montana's Ancient Order of Hibernians marched in a Saturday morning parade; a Hibernian banquet was held Saturday evening; and a traditional Catholic Mass was performed at the gazebo in Old Fort Park on Sunday morning, followed by the dedication of a new Thomas Francis Meagher Memorial on the historic steamboat levee. General Meagher, played by Francis Crowley of Helena, spoke at the dedication, while Governor Brian Schweitzer gave the main address. Following the speeches, the Thomas Francis Meagher Memorial was dedicated.

Today as you visit Fort Benton, you see a small, quiet river town with a big history. Look over Fort Benton from the bluffs and imagine the sights and sounds of the town in 1867 going full blast night and day. Imagine the long levee filled with steamboats, hundreds of tons of freight piled on

Monument to Acting Governor Thomas Francis Meagher on the Fort Benton Steamboat Levee. *Author's collection.*

the levee and hundreds of freight wagons and muleskinners filling the streets. When you walk the streets and tour the still standing I.G. Baker house, imagine the Irish general sitting there, eating his last meal. As you visit the Museum of the Upper Missouri, look at parts of two surviving arms shipment crates addressed to "His Excellency the Governor of Montana Territory" from the Federal arsenal at Frankfurt, Kentucky. As you walk the levee, imagine the two-hundred-foot steamboat *G.A. Thomson* moored alongside and General Meagher restless in his stateroom just before he stepped out the cabin door and off the deck into the cold, swirling current to his watery grave. Pause at the Thomas Francis Meagher Monument on the levee to pay homage to the exceptional Irish revolutionary hero, the brave Civil War leader of the Irish Brigade and the larger-than-life early Montana territorial saint and sinner. You are in Fort Benton, Montana—Meagher country!

FROM CONGRESS TO GOVERNOR OF MONTANA TERRITORY: ABOLITIONIST JAMES M. ASHLEY[3]

Our Civil War was fought on many fronts. The brilliant movie *Lincoln* by Steven Spielberg served a recent reminder that the conflict that began to preserve the Union evolved into a war against slavery and was fought as fiercely in the halls of Congress as on the battlefields. While President Abraham Lincoln's Emancipation Proclamation in 1863 freed slaves in

---

3. Earlier version published in *Great Falls Tribune* (hereafter *Tribune*), December 30, 2012.

areas of the Southern states controlled by Federal troops, it did not free all slaves throughout the Union. As a wartime measure, Lincoln believed his Proclamation might not survive postwar court challenges; thus, he perceived an urgent need for an amendment to the U.S. Constitution to permanently abolish slavery throughout the nation.

During the Civil War, Representative James M. Ashley, congressman from Ohio, introduced a bill to abolish slavery in the District of Columbia and initiated the first bill for a constitutional amendment abolishing slavery—and he led the charge in the House of Representatives to approve the antislavery Thirteenth Amendment. As floor manager of the bill, with strong support from President Lincoln and abolitionists in Congress, he skillfully managed to gain a narrow cliff-hanging two-thirds super-majority approval, as portrayed vividly in the movie *Lincoln*. In the words of historian Allen Guelzo, "Ashley went to work, lobbying queasy Republicans and nervous Democrats, backed by Lincoln's promise that 'whatever Ashley had promised should be performed.'" The amendment then went to the states for ratification by the end of 1865. The Thirteenth Amendment provided, "Neither slavery nor involuntary servitude…shall exist within the United States, or any place subject to their jurisdiction. Congress shall have power to enforce this article by appropriate legislation."

James M. Ashley, born near Pittsburgh, Pennsylvania, in 1822, moved with his family to Ohio in 1826. He became an ardent abolitionist, joining the new Republican Party in 1856. Ashley was elected to the House of Representatives from Ohio in 1858, and as chairman of the House Committee on Territories, on February 11, 1863, Ashley

Congressman James M. Ashley played the key role in forming Montana Territory but as governor couldn't govern it. *Library of Congress.*

reported a bill for the organization of Montana as a territory. The bill became law in 1864.

In January 1867, Representative Ashley moved resolutions and acted as prosecutor for the impeachment of President Andrew Johnson, an effort that failed by a single vote. After Ashley was defeated for reelection to Congress in 1868, President U.S. Grant named him governor of Montana Territory. He was confirmed by just a single vote because of the opposition of many Senate Democrats.

Governor James Ashley arrived in Helena, Montana Territory, during the summer of 1869 with high hopes that he would be able to convert the territory that he had created from a Democratic to a Republican majority. The Democratic press attacked Ashley ruthlessly from the moment he was appointed to the end of his tenure in Montana. The two previous governors had been Union Democrats more in tune with the territory's dominant Democratic sentiment. Pro-Confederate feeling remained far more than a myth in Montana, and it was not about to quietly accept staunch Unionist, Radical Republican Governor Ashley.

Governor Ashley faced a powerful Democratic majority in the sixth session of the territorial legislature—just three Republicans in the twenty-four-member House and none in the Council. Despite the Democratic dominance, Governor Ashley entertained no compromise. In his mind, a large portion of the population of Montana in 1869 was southern, anti-Negro and Democratic. The governor traveled around the territory to become acquainted with the people and their needs, yet he had a hard time working with the legislature.

Governor Ashley challenged the right of the legislature to meet in late 1869 since federal acts paved the way for biennial rather than annual sessions. The legislature met anyway. The Democrats demanded half the appointments to territorial offices, yet Ashley refused to appoint Democrats, and in turn, the legislature refused to confirm any of his appointments. The governor sent dozens of names to the legislature, yet none was accepted.

In the midst of this deadlocked government, Ashley appointed a black American to serve as notary public. Although appointee Johnson perhaps wisely declined to serve, the appointment further agitated pro-southern Democrats.

In mid-December 1869, President Grant suddenly removed Governor Ashley from office for unknown reasons. As a result of his brief, unsuccessful tenure as governor, historian Clark Spence wrote, "William Ashley was through politically, broken on Democratic rocks in Montana." Civil War Congressman Ashley named and created the Territory of Montana, but he couldn't govern it.

GETTYSBURG HERO AND TERRITORIAL MONTANA DELEGATE: MAJOR MARTIN MAGINNIS[4]

Captain Martin Maginnis, survivor of the charge of the 1st Minnesota Infantry Regiment at Gettysburg. *Author's collection.*

Martin Maginnis served with distinction in war and peace. Born of Irish parents in western New York on October 27, 1841, he moved to Minnesota with his family in 1852, attended Hamline University and became a newspaper editor at a young age. Early in the Civil War on April 18, 1861, in response to President Lincoln's first call for troops, Maginnis enlisted at Red Wing, Minnesota, and mustered in at Fort Snelling eleven days later, appointed sergeant in Company F 1st Minnesota Infantry Regiment. On July 21, 1861, the 1st Minnesota fought well despite the disastrous defeat of Union forces at the First Battle of Bull Run, and Maginnis was promoted to second lieutenant for his gallantry. Despite a severe wound to his left shoulder at Savage Station during the Seven Days Battle of the Peninsula Campaign in June 1862, he was assigned to command Company H and promoted to first lieutenant.

Lieutenant Maginnis and his 1st Minnesota Regiment participated in many of the Civil War's major battles, including First and Second Bull Run, Antietam and Gettysburg. In one of the most memorable events of the Civil War, the 1st Minnesota rose to legendary stature conducting a charge at Gettysburg in which 252 men went into action and just 47 came out unscathed. This charge resulted in the highest percentage of Union loss in any action of the war.

On July 2, 1863, Confederate brigadier general Cadmus M. Wilcox's men routed Major General Daniel Sickles's Third Corps. Flush with victory, the Southerners pursued the retreating Yankees to a point where Maginnis and his little band were positioned on the approach to Cemetery Ridge.

---

4. Earlier version published in *River Press*, May 29, 2013.

Major General Winfield Scott Hancock, making a frantic effort to rally his Union forces, dashed up and shouted out, "What regiment in this?" "The 1st Minnesota," was their colonel's reply.

"Charge those lines!" ordered Hancock, pointing to the Confederates. Although outnumbered about ten to one, the 1st Minnesota without hesitation fixed bayonets and charged. The ferocity of the onslaught of this band made up for their inferior numbers and shocked and stalled the Confederates, as their first line went down under the bayonets of the Minnesotans while the second line crumpled up from rifle fire that scorched their faces. The gallant charge was followed immediately by Union reserves. The Confederates broke and fled for cover. The day was saved; Hancock and the 1st Minnesota had held Cemetery Ridge to be hailed as heroes. Just Lieutenant Maginnis and two other officers out of twenty-four remained on their feet at the end of the battle, and in his company of thirty-five men, seventeen were killed and thirteen wounded.

In a lecture delivered later in life, Maginnis described the action of the 1st Minnesota on Cemetery Ridge on that day as they bravely conducted one of the most remarkable charges of the war. Maginnis's address, entitled "At Gettysburg The First Minnesota," was published in the *Gettysburg Star & Sentinel* on June 14, 1882:

> *The morning was foggy, sultry, and murky, and spent chiefly in skirmishing and desultory cannonading. The sharp-shooters on our front contested the right to hold the farm-houses, which were alternately occupied by either side, and finally burned...*[Major General Sickles moved his corps to an exposed forward position.]
>
> *Once there...cannon balls, shells, and bullets...went whistling and bursting above and around us, we beheld a grand sight. Below and before us on the plain the battle was fiercely raging. Every movement of the opposing troops were discernible, and we watched them with the anxiety of spectators so deeply interested in the result; though but little of this could be seen in the faces of our men, who, long accustomed to conceal their emotions beneath the mask of reckless indifference, were with apparent unconcern criticizing impartially the fighting of friend and foe.*
>
> *Soon the view became more obscured, for, though the sun shone brightly, the air was damp and the smoke hung heavily over the fight, sometimes in rolling, cloudy masses, and again, like a well-defined wall conforming to the lines of battle, rising high in the air. Through this could be seen the charging battalions, the darkened forms of the combatants, and the banners*

wildly tossing to and fro above the struggling masses, looming gigantically in the maze between us and the declining sun. Again the sulfurous pall would hide everything from view save when the flashes gleaming redly through the darkness revealed the position of the batteries, and we would intently listen, endeavoring to tell from the yelling and cheering which came up from the chaotic turmoil to which side the advantage leaned, while the rattle of small arms and the deep bass of the artillery made the music of the battle, and Round Top re-echoed the grand diapason. Then the breeze would roll up the smoky curtain, and none could repress a shout of joy to see that our men were still crowding the fight, and every heart felt the meaning of those expressive words of our national anthem, "Our flag is still there."

…[Sickles was wounded, and the divisions of his Third Corps broke under Confederate pressure.]

…The rebel batteries poured grape and canister into the retreating groups, and, their infantry advancing with triumphant yells, showered rapid volleys of leaden hail into the broken ranks, which were reeling and staggering back, but still turned to make fight, like some feeble but spirited man beneath the blows of a young and vigorous giant. Thomas' battery, which had necessarily been silent till these troops had cleared its front, now opened upon the rebel infantry at short range. This turned their attention to an objective point, and soon a group of crimson battle-flags were advancing through the smoke toward it, supported only as it was by eight companies of the 1ˢᵗ Minnesota—252 officers and men all told.

Just then Hancock rode up, and, unable to conceal his agitation, asked in almost anguished tones, "Great God! Is this all the men we have here?" And turned toward the right, from which was hastening Gen. Alpheus Williams' division, but still five minutes distant, and before they reached us the foe would have the battery and gain the very heart of the position. Not a hundred yards behind us was the road, crowded with our wagons, and beyond them the hospitals and trains. If Hancock could only stop that charging mass for five minutes. A hope lit up his face, and, pointing to the smoke-covered masses of the advancing foe, he cried: "Col. Colvill, advance and take those colors!"

It is an easy thing to charge when the enemy is retreating and the battle is going well, but it requires steady troops to even hold a position when the line is breaking away on every side, and it was a strange order to give a handful to charge that advancing mass that had just carried two of our best divisions off their feet…

"Forward!" shouted our gallant Colonel, and as one man the regiment arose, and, as if on review, stepped down the slope toward the enemy.

Their cannon opened on us, and shell and solid shot tore through the ranks, and the more deadly Enfield rifles of their infantry were centered on us alone. At every step fell our men, yet no one wavered; every gap is closed up, and bringing down their bayonets, the boys press shoulder to shoulder, and disdaining the factitious courage proceeding from noise or excitement, without word or cheer, but with silent desperate determination, step firmly forward. Five color-bearers are shot down, and five times our flag, proudly, goes forward as before.

"Steady they step down the slope, steadily down the hill.
Steadily load, and steadily fire, and march right onward still."

…Within a hundred ten of our men already fallen, and yet no shot has been fired at the enemy, whose foremost rank, consisting of Forney's, Herbert's, and other regiments of the Alabama brigade, commanded by Wilcox, and portions of Barksdale's brigade of Mississippians, all of whom had lost their order and alignment, had become mingled in one advancing mass during their fight with and pursuit of the Third Corps. Behind them in alignment came a body of troops, since understood to be a Florida brigade, which had not been actively engaged, but was supporting the victorious advance of their comrades. As soon as our movement was noticed the advancing mass stopped and opened a murderous fire upon us at not more than fifty yards' distance.

"Charge, men!" ran the order along the line, and with a wild cheer we ran at them. Their extended front swept around our flanks like the waters round a rock. But before us they gave way, for we empty our guns with the muzzles at their very hearts, and but little ammunition was wasted at that volley. A perfect swath of men sink upon the ground, and their living recoil back upon their second and third lines, and the body of many a chivalric Southerner lies beneath the feet of our men. Their supporting lines, confused and excited, wildly commence firing through the mass in front, slaughtering their own men by hundreds, and throwing the whole column into confusion, while their artillery from the rear fired on friends and foe alike. Their officers endeavored to stop the firing and restore order, and there, like some small obstacle thrown in the way of a locomotive to stop the power that will grind it to dust, we had momentarily checked the momentum of the mass, which in another moment would recover itself and sweep us from the earth; but the time had been gained, and at that instant a battery on our left opened, and poured a few rapid volleys into the confused mass, swept

it from the field; and before we had recovered from the shock we found ourselves among groups of disarmed prisoners, and our bewildered senses take in the fact that the enemy have somehow disappeared from the plain, all but his dead and wounded, and over their prostrate bodies ring the hearty cheers of our reinforcing troops.

That is the manner and order in which these things happened, as I have been told by those whose position made them lookers-on. For who that was an actor there can give the order or detail the changes of the eventful and exciting moments following that word "Charge"? When we heard neither ball not shell now saw our comrades fall; when the blood rushed like fire through the distended veins and every faculty was absorbed in the one desire to conquer or to die—no, not to die...

The almost fatal attack was repulsed; but where was the First Minnesota? Had they deserted the field for the first time? That was the first idea that came to my senses, half oblivious of what had passed. But forty-seven men now gathered round the colors. Great heavens, is it possible that the other two hundred five lie bleeding under them? Yes, they are all there within a hundred square yards of crimson sward—two hundred and five killed, wounded, and none missing...

It was indeed the Thermopylae of the Regiment. Our colonel, lieutenant colonel, major, and adjutant were all wounded, each mortally, as was the feared, for all were pierced with more than one ball, which was the case with most of the wounded, and some of the corpses were perfectly riddled and few escaped without a scratch. Out of twenty-one line officers but five were fit for duty. The command devolved upon Capt. N.S. Messick, and, as the senior lieutenant, I acted as his adjutant, turned over five men left of my company of thirty-five that morning, thirteen being killed and seventeen wounded, to another lieutenant.

In the aftermath of Gettysburg, on July 29, 1863, Maginnis was promoted to captain. The 1st Minnesota was discharged in May 1864. Four months later, Captain Maginnis joined the new 11th Minnesota Infantry to serve as quartermaster as that regiment operated under Major General George H. Thomas's division in the Army of the Cumberland. One month later, Maginnis was promoted to major and served until June 26, 1865, when he was mustered out.

In 1866, Maginnis emigrated overland with the Henry B. Steele party from Minnesota to Montana Territory to try his hand at mining. Two years later, he became an intensely partisan democratic editor of the *Rocky*

Mountain Gazette newspaper in Helena. In August 1871, Maginnis narrowly defeated incumbent Republican William H. Claggett to become Montana's non-voting territorial delegate in Congress, where he served for twelve years. During his congressional years, Delegate Maginnis made an impressive record, convincing Congress to build Forts Custer, Keogh, Logan and Maginnis, improving navigation on the Missouri River, opening reservation land to white settlement and encouraging railroad building to promote settlement—all measures designed to increase the territory's population.

Maginnis was elected to the state constitutional convention in 1889 but defeated for the U.S. Senate that same year in a disputed partisan election. Major Martin Maginnis, who served Minnesota and the nation with distinction in the Civil War and Montana well as territorial delegate in Congress, spent the last four years of his life in California and died on March 27, 1919, in Los Angeles. He rests today in Resurrection Cemetery in Helena.

REPUBLICAN MAN OF STEEL: COLONEL WILBUR FISK SANDERS

Fearless and committed, young Wilbur Fisk Sanders arrived in Bannack, eastern Idaho Territory, in September 1863 with his uncle Sidney Edgerton. Within three months of his arrival, Sanders's name became a respected household word for his successful prosecution of road agent and murderer George Ives. In the face of strong pressure and threats from friends of Ives and Sheriff Henry Plummer, Sanders stood strong. Protected by Captain Nick Wall and his men, Sanders and Wall with three fellow Masons met and organized the first vigilante movement.

Wilbur Fisk Sanders was born in Leon, New York, on May 2, 1834. At age twenty, he moved to Akron, Ohio, where he taught school and studied law. He was admitted to the bar in 1856, and early in the Civil War, he recruited a company of infantry and a battery of artillery and was commissioned first lieutenant in the 64th Ohio Infantry. Serving also as adjutant, his unit constructed defenses along the railroads south of Nashville. When his term of enlistment expired in October 1862, he left the army.

Arriving in lawless eastern Idaho, Sanders and his family settled with the Edgertons in the booming mining camp of Bannack and began to practice law. As he acquired money, he invested in mining and stock raising. These

Wilbur Fisk Sanders, vigilante prosecutor and
Montana Territory's Republican Warhorse.
Author's collection.

were the days before courts were
organized in pre-territorial Montana.
Dozens of men carrying gold were
ambushed and murdered in the
Bannack and Virginia City areas
by an organized gang led by Sheriff
Henry Plummer. Only Sanders
stepped forward to prosecute
accused murderer George Ives. This
led to the hanging of Ives and the rest
of Plummer's "road agents" to end the
reign of terror in the new gold camps.

His courage during the Ives trial and the
subsequent vigilante actions gained Sanders
the respect and admiration of most residents.
In the face of predominant Democrat sentiment in the new territory, ardent
Lincoln Republican Sanders ran unsuccessfully for delegate to Congress in the
elections of 1864, 1867, 1880 and 1886.

More successful at the local level, Sanders served in the Territorial House
of Representatives from 1873 to 1879. Throughout the early decades, win
or lose, Sanders was Mr. Republican in Montana Territory. Upon admission
of Montana as a state in the fall of 1889, Sanders was elected to the United
States Senate and served from January 1, 1890, to March 3, 1893. The
election in which both Republicans Sanders and Thomas C. Power were
elected to the Senate was hotly contested and set the stage for Sanders's
defeat for reelection.

Throughout his years in Montana, Sanders often took the side of the
unpopular underdog as a champion of the downtrodden, defending native
Indians like the Blackfoot Spo-pee, in his murder trial. With his wife, Harriet,
Sanders promoted the career of Helen Clarke, the mixed-race daughter of
fur trader Malcolm Clarke and his Piegan Blackfoot wife, recruiting her to
teach in the Helena schools and later to run successfully for superintendent
of schools in Lewis and Clark County. Sanders won an injunction against a
labor union seeking to exclude Chinese workers. He supported equal rights

for black Americans and defended them in court, while Harriet was a leader in the 1890s Political Equality Clubs that narrowly failed to bring women's suffrage to Montana in 1894. Wilbur Sanders strongly supported his cousin Martha Edgerton Rolfe when she became the first female editor of a daily newspaper, the *Great Falls Leader*, upon the death of her husband.

The old soldier, vigilante and Republican war horse died in Helena on July 7, 1905, and was interred in Forestvale Cemetery.

Chapter 3

Profiles in Courage

Civil War Officers and Enlisted Soldiers

Among the thousands of combat veterans who came to Montana Territory after the Civil War, those presented here show the many sides of war and peace and the battles fought in both Western and Eastern Theaters. Private J.O. Gregg received the Medal of Honor for his valor during the war and became an important leader in the GAR in Montana. Tough as nails Confederate sharpshooter Robert Chesnut left his mark and name on Montana. "Moss Backed Yankee" private Robert Craven served the Lord for decades after the war. Larger-than-life Colonel John Donnelly served with distinction during the Civil War, led Fenian invasions of Canada after the war and left a distinguished record of accomplishment in Montana before his bizarre death in the Missouri River. Young John Byrd fought briefly in bloody Missouri under General Sterling Price before becoming one of the many men of Price's Army to head west to Montana Territory. For every Civil War veteran, there is a story with many more to write.

MEDAL OF HONOR: PRIVATE JOSEPH O. GREGG[5]

Private Joseph O. Gregg, Montana's first Medal of Honor recipient, received his award for service in the Civil War while living in Great Falls, Montana.

---

5. Earlier version published in *Tribune*, December 25, 2011.

His award is credited to Ohio since he entered military service in that state, yet after the war, he became one of Montana's most important veterans.

Joseph Olds "J.O." Gregg was born on January 5, 1841, in Circleville, Ohio. As a twenty-year-old clerk working in his father's dry goods store, Gregg enlisted in Company I, 28th Ohio Infantry Regiment, on December 13, 1861. Promoted to corporal, he received a disability discharge in July 1862. His health improved by May 1864, and he enlisted in Company F, 133rd Ohio Infantry Regiment. One month later, while his regiment was engaged in combat near the Richmond & Petersburg Railway in Virginia, Private Gregg volunteered for a dangerous mission: to return to breastworks that his outnumbered regiment had been forced to abandon. His mission was to warn three missing companies that the regiment was falling back. Private Gregg crossed an open field under fire, found the enemy already in the breastworks, refused a demand to surrender and returned to his command under a concentrated fire, with several bullets passing through his hat and clothing.

J.O. Gregg came to Great Falls in 1888 from Fargo, Dakota Territory. For sixteen years, Great Falls had a soldier of war and peace known as "Captain Gregg." On his arrival, he invested in the development of the North Great Falls Townsite. Yet most of his time and energy went into veteran affairs. He served as commander of Great Falls Sheridan Post No. 18 of the Grand Army of the Republic; department commander of the Montana GAR, 1892–94; national leader in the GAR; vice-commander of the national Congressional Medal of Honor Legion; and member of the Army and Navy Legion.

In the early 1890s, Captain Gregg promoted an idea that was later copied by many other cities in America. Thus, Great Falls has

Joseph O. Gregg wearing his Congressional Medal of Honor and Grand Army of the Republic insignia. *Montana Historical Society.*

the distinction of having the first burial plot in the United States on which a monument was dedicated jointly to both Union and Confederate soldiers of the Civil War. Veterans Plot in Highland Cemetery, with its Soldiers Monument, is a national memorial.

In April 1899, a letter arrived in Great Falls from the secretary of war notifying Private Joseph O. Gregg that he had been awarded the Medal of Honor "for most distinguished gallantry in action, while a member of Company F, 133d regiment, Ohio infantry...June 16, 1864." In the words of his regimental adjutant:

> *We saw [Private Gregg] mount the breastworks...then run along the crest about 100 feet to the left and suddenly spring from the embankment over which a large number of men in gray could be seen leaping in an effort to head off his retreat, while many others were firing at close range at their active young foeman, who, dodging with zigzag rushes to avoid the blows aimed at his head...successfully made his escape to our lines, all the while under a concentrated fire, several balls having passed through his cap and clothing, but without injury to his person...We considered it a truly remarkable exhibition of daring. Alone, surrounded by hundreds of Pickett's best marksmen...and ordered to surrender, Gregg's quick decision and prompt, bold action, together with his skill...enabled him to escape with life and limb, when to us who were watching his struggle there did not seem to be a chance in his favor.*

Gregg's colonel greeted him by saying, "That was bravely done; you must have been under special protection of Providence."

During the Civil War, no other military medal was authorized, and this explains why the Medal of Honor was awarded for some seemingly less notable actions when judged by today's standards. The criteria for the award tightened after World War I. Overall, 1,522 Medals of Honor were awarded for Civil War service, and many of these were awarded decades after the war, such as Private Gregg's award in 1899. Twenty-five African Americans earned the Medal of Honor during the Civil War, including seven sailors of the Union navy.

Private Joseph O. Gregg's leadership in the GAR and his successful efforts to designate Veterans Plot at Highland Cemetery and to erect a unique Soldiers Monument dedicated to both the blue and the gray remain unexcelled in Montana veteran affairs. He was a brave soldier, a Medal of Honor hero and a valued Montanan.

Joseph O. Gregg left Great Falls early in 1904 to stump Ohio for President Teddy Roosevelt's presidential campaign. While in his home state, Gregg met and married a wealthy cousin of Senator Mark Hanna and settled there. In March 1930, at age ninety, Gregg was struck and killed instantly by an automobile in Columbus, Ohio. With the death of Joseph O. Gregg, Montana and Ohio lost a good man and one who proudly wore the Medal of Honor.

Confederate Sharpshooter: Robert Chesnut[6]

Bob Chesnut was no angel, and he never claimed to be. Captain Robert Chesnut, 6th Texas Cavalry, was a sharpshooter and tough as nails. He fought the good fight for his cause, the Confederate States of America.

Chesnut was born in 1835 in the mountains of Clay County, Kentucky. Historian Charles House states, "Robert grew up in a singularly violent place" with mountain feuding that could be traced in part back to the Civil War. The Chesnut families were Democrats in a heavily Republican county. Family lore remembers Bob as "a troublesome sort, unusually independent." He became a crack shot hunting wild turkeys and squirrels with a long-barrel, muzzleloading rifle. As war neared, Robert became a passionate defender of the Southern cause.

Chesnut enlisted in Company A, 6th Texas Cavalry, on August 10, 1861, when mounted residents of North Texas formed the regiment. Confederate war records are incomplete, but Captain Robert Chestnut's service is documented in several unusual ways. His name and those of many other Confederates inadvertently were recorded and then crossed out in the Union Veteran Schedule of the 1890 U.S. Census for Montana's Cascade County: "Robert Chesnut 1861–64 Captain

Confederate sharpshooter Robert Chesnut, 6th Texas Cavalry. *Charles House Collection.*

6. Earlier version published in *Tribune*, November 27, 2011.

Company A, 6th Texas, enlisted 10 Aug 1861 discharged 1 Aug 1864 served 2 years 11 months 21 days. Born July 1835 KY. Single. Prospector."

The 6th Texas Cavalry, known as the Sharp Shooters, served in more than eighty-five skirmishes, engagements and battles, including Pea Ridge, Holly Springs, and the Atlanta Campaign. They slipped behind Union lines, provided intelligence and disrupted Union supply lines. The 6th roamed widely through the Indian territories, border states and South, often broken into smaller elements supporting operations by Generals Nathan Bedford Forrest and Sterling "Pap" Price. The Sharp Shooters gained fame as a fighting unit, though at the cost of heavy casualties.

Captain Chesnut was discharged on August 1, 1864, but he remained a proud Confederate for the rest of his days. Twenty years later, while spending Christmas at the Robert Thoroughman home near Cascade, Montana, Chesnut was invited by young Joe Thoroughman to sign his new autograph book. Chesnut wrote:

Captain Robert Chesnut
Company A
6th Texas Cavalry Sharp Shooters, C.S.A.

Later, Joe Thoroughman wrote, "That is the way he wrote it in my autograph album. He told me that he was one of Quantril's Gorillas [*sic*], engaged in what he called border warfare."

After his war ended, Chesnut tried to return to Kentucky, but neither neighbors nor family welcomed him. He drifted West, freighting from Leavenworth, Kansas, with ox teams, soon becoming a wagon master.

By 1865, Bob Chesnut had arrived in Montana Territory, drifting into the valley that almost bears his name along the east side of the Missouri River near today's town of Cascade. The valley and post office were named for Robert Chesnut, but bureaucracy imposed the name "Chestnut" on both, much to Robert's chagrin. Joe Thoroughman recalled Chesnut complaining, "When you put 't' in the middle of my name, you make a nut out of it, and by God, I'm no damn nut!"

Bob Chesnut was a picturesque character following the life of a trapper and hunter. Old-timer Fisk G. Ellis recalled, "He was a fine specimen of physical manhood; tall, erect, well built and weighing about 180 pounds. His face was broad, well proportioned, swarthy, with a kindly expression. Hair and mustache were iron gray."

Robert Chesnut standing by his cabin in Chestnut Valley holding his rifle.
Wedsworth Memorial Library, Cascade, Montana.

Bob Chesnut left a trail of stories that could extend from Cascade to Great Falls (some thirty miles). His Kentucky family received a letter from him postmarked Sun River, Montana, June 16, 1888: "If there is any good looking olde maids or Rich Widows without Children pleas Recomende me to them tell them that I am a Rebel and a drinking Sorte of a Connection and a good fidler & a hell of a fellow generly—and if any of them likes the Recomend tell them to Write me a long letter—giving her name pedigree etc. R.C." No letters apparently came.

Among the memorable stories is that of Orrin G. "Yank" Robie, a neighbor of "Rebel" Chesnut. Robie was found dead in his cabin in 1897 with two bullets in the back of his head. A coroner's jury concluded that his death came "by a shot from a 50-caliber needle gun in the hands of a person unknown." Despite the verdict, some neighbors believed Chesnut was the murderer, though he was never charged.

Chesnut remained in Chestnut Valley until 1901, when he returned home to Clay County, Kentucky. In the spring of 1905, he suffered a paralytic stroke and died on October 18, 1912. Montana lost a passionate Confederate veteran.

AN EXCEPTIONAL WARRIOR: PRIVATE JAMES W. "DIAMOND R" BROWN[7]

James W. Brown II was a survivor. Wounded in three major battles, he survived the war and came west to Montana Territory to become a legendary freighting wagon boss on the rugged Montana frontier.

Brown was born in Hillsboro, Ohio, on September 5, 1841. His parents, James W. and Elizabeth Cooper Brown, both of Pennsylvania Dutch ancestry, had earlier moved from Virginia to Ohio. His father died in 1850, and after attending school in Hillsboro, young James left home in 1858 to work as a farmhand in Illinois. At the call for troops in the Civil War, James Brown enlisted on June 13, 1861, at Joliet, Illinois, for a term of three years as private in Company C, 20th Illinois Infantry. He was twenty-one years of age with hazel eyes and dark hair. Brown served from June 1861 until July 1864 through extended periods of hard fighting in the Western Theater.

Fort Donelson was located on the left bank of the vital Cumberland River in a strategic position in northwestern Tennessee. It was a bastioned earthwork on a bluff about one hundred feet above the water and commanded the river for several miles downstream. During February 13–16, 1862, a twenty-seven-thousand-man army under Brigadier General Ulysses S. Grant, supported by ironclad gunboats under Commodore Andrew Foote, attacked and captured Fort Donelson.

---

7. Earlier version published in *River Press*, March 21, March 28, 2012.

Shortly after daybreak on February 16, the notes of a bugle were heard in the direction of the fort, announcing the approach of an officer with a communication from Confederate brigadier general Simon B. Buckner, asking for an armistice until noon and the appointment of commissioners to agree on the terms of capitulation. It was then that General Ulysses S. Grant sent his famous message: "No terms except an unconditional and immediate surrender can be accepted. I propose to move immediately upon your works." Thus was born the famed "Unconditional Surrender Grant."

Buckner was forced to comply, surrendering more than twelve thousand men, and the Union forces marched in and took possession. In this battle, Brigadier General Gideon Pillow and cavalry Colonel Nathan B. Forrest refused to surrender, and about three thousand Confederates escaped in the early morning hours. The most important result of the fall of Fort Donelson was the opening of the Cumberland River to the passage of the Union gunboats and transports, and that broke the line of defense to Nashville.

With the fall of Forts Henry and Donelson, Confederate general Albert Sidney Johnston, commander in the area, was forced to fall back, giving up Kentucky and much of western and middle Tennessee. Private James Brown was wounded during the capture of Fort Donelson, but his wounds did not keep him out of action seven weeks later when the 20th Illinois Infantry was again part of Major General John A. McClernand's First Division as General Grant's Army of Tennessee arrived at Pittsburgh Landing on the west bank of the Tennessee River. The army camped and awaited the arrival of Major General Don Carlos Buell's army (expected late the next day) before moving on. The Union forces did not set up defenses or even send out pickets since no Confederates were believed to be nearby.

Unknown to the Union forces, Confederate general Albert Sidney Johnston had assembled his Army of Mississippi and was moving north to intercept and destroy Grant's army and capture his supplies before Buell's army arrived. The battle began early on April 6 with the Confederate forces streaming out of the woods and surprising the Union troops. Grant's army fell back before the attackers but put up stubborn resistance at a sunken road known later as the Hornet's Nest. The determined resistance at the Hornet's Nest threw off the timetable of the advancing Confederates and likely saved the rest of Grant's army. During the fighting, General Johnston was killed while leading his troops, and command fell to General P.G.T. Beauregard. By the end of the day, the Confederates had pushed the Union army back into a small pocket next to the river where the Union gunboats could offer some protection.

During the night, General Buell's Army of the Ohio arrived, and the troops were ferried across the river to the west bank. At the end of that bloody day, Major General William T. Sherman approached General Grant, who was smoking one of his cigars. "Well, Grant, we've had the devil's own day, haven't we?" General Grant looked up. "Yes," he replied, followed by a puff. "Yes. Lick 'em tomorrow, though." Meanwhile, Confederate general Beauregard completely misread the situation, sending a telegram to President Jefferson Davis announcing, "A COMPLETE VICTORY."

At daybreak on April 7, the newly reinforced Union army attacked and over the course of the day completely pushed the Confederates back across the battlefield of the previous day. The Confederates were forced to retreat in the bloodiest battle to date, ending hopes that they could block the Union advance into northern Mississippi. The Battle of Shiloh or Pittsburgh Landing was the first of many large battles during the war to have in excess of twenty thousand casualties and was an omen that the war would last much longer and be far bloodier than anticipated.

One year later, the 20th Illinois Infantry joined in the extended Vicksburg Campaign from May 18 to July 4, a series of maneuvers and battles against Vicksburg, a fortress city that dominated the last Confederate-controlled section of the Mississippi River. Grant's Army of Tennessee captured this stronghold and the thirty-thousand-man Confederate forces stationed there.

This was the second major blow to the Confederacy in the summer of 1863, in the same week that General Robert E. Lee's invasion of the North collapsed at Gettysburg. On July 4, the Stars and Stripes rose over Vicksburg. The most significant result of this campaign was control of the Mississippi River—the Confederacy was now cut in two. One week later, an unarmed steamboat arrived in Union-held New Orleans from St. Louis after an uneventful trip down the river. President Lincoln announced, "The Father of Waters again goes unvexed to the sea."

Private James Brown was wounded for the third time at Vicksburg. He was discharged in July 1864 at Nashville, Tennessee. Remarkably, he had not had enough of war, and in February 1865, he reenlisted for a year in the 4th Veteran Regiment of General Winfield S. Hancock's First Veterans Corps to provide security for the Federal capital. Private Brown was in camp at Alexandria, Virginia, across the Potomac River, at the time of the assassination of President Lincoln on April 14, 1865. His regiment was immediately placed on provost duty in Washington and continued that service until after July 7, 1865, the day of execution for Mrs. Mary Surratt and the other conspirators convicted of complicity in that tragedy. In the fall of 1865, Private James Brown returned to Ohio to muster out of service on February 7, 1866. Wounded but unbowed, he had survived the Civil War.

In February 1866, this exceptional man of adventure headed west. Engaged as a bullwhacker driving an oxen team between Nebraska City and Salt Lake City, he arrived there in August and immediately loaded freight for Helena, Montana Territory. Reaching Helena in September, he sold his ox team to Carroll, Steell & Hubbell and in exchange was hired as wagon master. His first trip was to St. Peter's Mission to load his teams with hay for the new military post Camp Cooke at the mouth of Judith River. The $125 per ton he received from the army at Camp Cooke would be worth a stunning $1,838 per ton today.

At Camp Cooke, Brown loaded with government freight for Fort Benton and made two trips during the fall. The next February, he was engaged by I.G. Baker & Co. to take a pack train with provisions for Fort Hawley on the Missouri River twenty miles above the mouth of the Musselshell River.

The return trip to Camp Cooke was made through heavy snowstorms and severe cold, and there he found the soldiers in a deplorable condition. Indians had killed a sentinel the night before. Commanding officer Major William Clinton had tried for several days to get mail through to Benton, but the party returned with several men badly frozen. Brown took on the challenge, guiding a party through safely to Benton in two days. The weather was intensely cold, the river being frozen to the depth of four feet. With the thermometer so low and a terrific ice-cold blizzard raging over the wide sweep of level country, old-timers who had experience understood what this trip from Camp Cooke to Fort Benton must have been like. No amount of clothing kept them warm, yet under Brown's leadership they made it to Benton.

In the spring of 1867, John J. Roe & Company, the Diamond R, hired James Brown to move government stores from Fort Benton to Fort Shaw. During the fall, he transferred freight from Fort Shaw to Fort Ellis, thence going to Fort Hawley for oats left there by a stranded steamboat. For protection from attack by Indians, Brown armed his train with two small cannon and an arsenal of small arms.

The following year, Matthew Carroll, George Steell and C.A. Broadwater bought the Diamond R, and from that point on the moniker "Diamond R" Brown was born. That year, Brown married Sarah Bull, daughter of Piegan Blackfeet Melting Marrow (Bull) and Bird Sailing This Way, in Fort Benton in the "Indian custom." Later in 1888–89, a priest at Holy Family Mission blessed this marriage. Sarah had been born at the Fort Benton trading post in May 1854. She became mother to seven children and died on December 3, 1912, at Browning.

In the spring of 1869, Brown located a ranch at Eight-Mile Springs near Fort Benton, but ranch life was not for him. He remained with the Diamond R until 1870, when he formed a partnership with trader Joe Kipp. Going into Canada over the Whoop-Up Trail, Kipp and Brown built a trading post on the Belly River.

Two years later, Brown and Kipp erected Fort Kipp at the mouth of Old Man's River and another at High River, where they traded profitably with the Blackfoot, supplying them with goods brought from Fort Benton in exchange for bison robes. In the summer of 1874, Diamond R Brown began trading on his own account at Old Man's River, Canada, and from 1875 to 1881 was in the service of merchant Tom C. Power as manager of Kipp's trading post.

In 1890, Brown and his family moved to Choteau, where he served for three years as assistant farmer at the Blackfeet Old Agency. In 1893, he secured a ranch of one thousand acres on the South Fork of the Milk River on the Blackfeet reservation, where he raised cattle and racehorses. After his wife passed away, Brown moved to Browning and made his home with daughter Geneva.

Historical writer Martha Edgerton Plassmann visited Browning in 1925 to write a biography of Brown. Mrs. Plassmann wrote of Brown's marriage, "He married a Piegan woman, and by her had several children. Unlike some others in the northwest, the influx of the whites did not lead him to put away the mother of his children to take a white wife—on the contrary he remained true to her until her death a few years ago, and by so doing earned the respect of all right-thinking persons."

James W. "Diamond R" Brown II passed away on December 23, 1927, in Browning. He lived a life of adventure and hardship,

James W. Brown, Company K, 4th U.S. Infantry. Gravestone at St. Michael's Cemetery on the Blackfeet Indian Reservation, Browning, Montana. *Author's collection.*

surviving wounds from the Civil War and the many dangers of the harsh life of an overland freighter on the Montana frontier. His memory lives on through many descendants and the striking image of old Diamond R Brown guiding his wagon train up the bluffs from Fort Benton in Charles M. Russell's powerful tribute to the overland freighters, the painting *Wagon Boss*.

A "Moss Backed Yankee" in a Rebel Uniform: Private Robert M. Craven[8]

Robert Martin Craven was born on November 7, 1842, in cotton-growing Colleton County, South Carolina. Robert's father was a Unionist small planter of Scot descent who worked his land in competition with plantation slave labor. His mother, a Connecticut Yankee, died early, leaving seven children. Family members were viewed as traitors or "mossbacks" when the war began. Young Craven fought for both sides during the Civil War, and that put him on the wrong side of the fence in both North and South. Yet Robert Craven achieved striking success as a force for good in frontier Montana.

Craven's early years working on the farm limited his education. Apprenticed as a carpenter, the outbreak of the War for Southern Independence changed his life. In August 1861, eighteen-year-old Robert Craven joined the Colleton Guards, 11th South Carolina Infantry. Craven remained with the 11th until May 16, 1864, when he was captured near Richmond during the Battle of Drury's Bluff and sent to prison camp.

At Point Lookout Prison, Craven opted to enlist for three years in the Union Army's new 1st U.S. Volunteer Infantry formed by Confederate prisoners of war. The 1st U.S. Volunteer, known as "Galvanized Yankees," was sent up the Missouri River to garrison Fort Rice in Dakota Territory during the Sioux Indian Wars. Private Craven served as post librarian and company clerk until September 1865, when he was hospitalized in St. Louis and then discharged from service.

Robert Craven's wars were over, and at age twenty-two, he struck out for Leavenworth, Kansas, where he found work building Fort Leavenworth. During this time, he converted to the Methodist Episcopal Church. Working hard and saving his money, in 1868 he took passage on the steamboat *Columbia* to Fort Benton. Working as a carpenter in Helena, Craven helped

---

8. Earlier version published in *Tribune*, April 29, 2012.

build the Southern Methodist Church, and in 1870, he married Miss Mary E. Frazier of Ohio.

While working at his building trade, Craven pursed religious studies, and in 1871, the Methodist Church South licensed him as preacher, becoming the first to be licensed to preach in Montana. The next year, the Cravens became friends with newly arrived William Wesley Van Orsdel or "Brother Van." Moving to full-time ministry, Craven was admitted to the Western Conference of the Southern Methodist Church and in 1876 was ordained deacon. Three years later, he was ordained elder and worked in the Gallatin Valley. An epidemic took three of the Cravens' children, and Robert was forced to leave the ministry for almost a decade as he worked to pay off debts.

In 1887, Craven returned to the ministry with the Northern Methodist Church. Jacob Mills, a Union army veteran, was presiding elder of the Bozeman District, and he and Craven, the son of the Confederacy, met and became lifelong friends. The fact that they had once been enemies in war made no difference. In a Decoration Day speech at the Great Falls Opera House in 1895, Craven expressed his feelings: "There are those who do not seem to know that the war is over, but they are not numbered among those who fought with the gun and the saber; their fight is by means of the ink bottle."

Reverend Craven held many pastorates in Montana, including Belt, Kalispell, West Side Great Falls, Fort Benton, Sand Coulee and Columbia Falls. He served as presiding elder of the Lewistown District and superintendent of the Kalispell Mission.

Confederate private, Galvanized Yankee and Methodist minister Robert Craven passed away on June 27, 1919, at Columbia Falls. In the cemetery is a large pine tree that he and his wife often admired. At his request, he was buried at its foot, and later Mrs. Craven was placed at his side. Brother Van eulogized his friend with these words:

> *Know ye not that there is a prince and a great man fallen this day in Israel,*
> *Servant of God well done*
> *Thy glorious welfare's past,*
> *The battles fought, the victory's won, and thou art crowned at last.*

LARGER-THAN-LIFE FRONTIER CHARACTER: COLONEL JOHN J. DONNELLY[9]

Frontier Fort Benton was a town of many colorful characters, but they broke the mold with John J. Donnelly. In the span of six decades, Colonel Donnelly fought with distinction through the Civil War; led Irish Fenian army invasions of Canada; organized a civilian army in the Nez Perce War; served as Fenian agitator, Louis Riel advisor and attorney; and worked as county clerk and recorder, probate judge and Speaker of the Montana House of Representatives. After this extraordinary career, even at the end he died a spectacular death.

Who was this man of triumph and tragedy in frontier Montana? John J. Donnelly was born on November 15, 1838, in Providence, Rhode Island, of Irish immigrant parents. He was educated at the College of the Holy Cross in Worcester, Massachusetts. Moving west to Michigan, he studied law in Detroit and was admitted to practice in November 1860.

One year later, young John J. Donnelly enlisted in the service of the United States and raised an infantry company. Named captain of Company G, his 14th Michigan Infantry was mustered into service on February 13, 1862, at Ypsilanti, Michigan. The 14th left Michigan in April for St. Louis and joined General Grant's army at Shiloh. It participated in the siege of Corinth, Mississippi, and when the enemy evacuated, the 14th joined General Buell's army in a race with the Confederates to Louisville, Kentucky.

At Nashville, Tennessee, the 14th Michigan was assigned to the First Brigade, Second Division, Fourteen Corps of the Army of the Cumberland, and served in that corps for the rest of the war. In

Civil War veteran and Irish Fenian leader John J. Donnelly cut a wide swath on the upper Missouri. *From Leeson's History of Montana, 1739–1885.*

---

9. Earlier version published in *River Press*, January 25, 2012.

November, the regiment had a sharp encounter with Alabama troops at Lavergne, Tennessee, when the 14th Michigan captured a fort and many prisoners.

Captain Donnelly led Company G until he was appointed engineering officer on the staff of Major General George H. Thomas, commander of Fourteen Corps. Promoted to lieutenant colonel, Donnelly served with General Thomas during 1863–64, while Thomas was gaining fame with his stout defense at the Battle of Chickamauga, saving the Union army from being routed and earning his nickname of respect, the "Rock of Chickamauga." General Thomas followed soon after with a dramatic breakthrough on Missionary Ridge in the Battle of Chattanooga, and in the Franklin-Nashville Campaign of 1864 he achieved one of the most decisive victories of the war, destroying the army of Confederate general John Bell Hood at the Battle of Nashville.

By 1864, Major General John M. Palmer had taken command of Fourteen Corps, and on August 5, Lieutenant Colonel Donnelly was promoted to full aide-de-camp on General Palmer's staff. In the Civil War, an aide-de-camp was a confidential officer appointed to the staff of a general officer, reporting directly to his commander and taking orders only from him. In a position of great responsibility, an aide was required to write orders, deliver them personally and be thoroughly knowledgeable about troop positions, maneuvers, columns, orders of corps and routes.

Fourteen Corps performed effectively in the Battle of Atlanta, Sherman's March to the Sea and actions to capture Savannah, Georgia, in late 1864. During Sherman's March, Colonel Donnelly was appointed assistant general superintendent of the military railway service in Sherman's department.

Throughout the war until his discharge on March 14, 1865, Colonel Donnelly took part in many of the principal engagements and was twice wounded, at Corinth and Resaca. One obituary read, "A braver soldier never drew his sword in any cause, and such is the testimonial of his superior officers and of the men who served under him."

As the Civil War drew to a close, Treasury Secretary Salmon P. Chase appointed Colonel Donnelly special agent of the Treasury Department. During Reconstruction days, he settled all war claims against the United States government in the Carolinas and part of Georgia and handled enormous sums of money without any suspicion of malfeasance. He also engaged in the wholesale grocery and commission business at Savannah, Georgia. In 1866, Colonel Donnelly closed out his business and came north to Michigan after the death of his wife.

Entering a new phase, Colonel Donnelly plunged headlong into the Irish Fenian movement, then at its highest strength. He became one of the most prominent figures in the subsequent "invasions" of Canada. The Fenian Brotherhood was an Irish republican organization founded in the United States in 1858 by John O'Mahony and Michael Doheny to punish the English for their occupation of Ireland. The Fenians dreamed of capturing Canada, forcing the English to free Ireland in exchange for the return of Canada. O'Mahony, a Celtic scholar, named his organization after the Fianna, the legendary band of Irish warriors led by Fionn mac Cumhaill.

With many other Irish Civil War veterans, Colonel Donnelly joined the Fenian invasions of Canada. A thousand-strong force of Fenians took the field in June 1866, crossed the Niagara River into Ontario, defeated a company of the Queen's Own Rifles of Toronto and captured Fort Erie. Shortly afterward, the Battle of Pigeon Hill practically ended this outbreak. In this battle, Colonel Donnelly led 200 men and was able to hold his position throughout the day against 2,300 English opposing him. He had 12 men killed and 17 wounded, with Donnelly among those wounded. He was captured but escaped, and a large reward was offered for him.

After the defeat at Pigeon Hill, Colonel Donnelly drifted westward and played a role in the Red River Rebellion of 1870, in which Louis Riel was leader of the Metis and Cree. This rebellion collapsed, as did another Fenian raid north of Pembina, Dakota Territory, the following year. Donnelly came to Montana from Pembina in 1872 and settled in Fort Benton to practice law.

In Fort Benton, Colonel John J. Donnelly became a spokesman for the many Irish Democrats of the town. Donnelly played a prominent part in the aftermath of the Cypress Hill Massacre of 1873; two years later, federal officials arrested five Bentonites accused of participating in the massacre for an extradition hearing in Helena. The so-called extradition prisoners were released and, upon their triumphant return to Fort Benton, were welcomed home by Colonel Donnelly with an eloquent speech condemning the attempted extradition.

In September 1877, when Chief Joseph's Nez Perce turned north toward the Missouri River in their flight to Canada, Colonel Donnelly, warrior and leader of men, raised a company of fifty civilian mounted volunteers to hasten down the Missouri to Cow Island. The men of Donnelly's company were tough, experienced in the hard and dangerous life of frontier Montana. At least four, and likely more, of Donnelly's men had extensive Civil War service; three had recently served in the 7th Infantry; and three were army scouts.

Donnelly's company arrived at Cow Island just after the Nez Perce had crossed the Missouri, fought a skirmish there and were moving up Cow Creek. On September 27, 1877, Donnelly's men engaged elements of the Nez Perce in a three-hour battle, with one man, black American Edmund Bradley, killed. Fortunately for Donnelly's company, the main Nez Perce camp was moving northward to meet its fate at Snake Creek in the Battle of the Bear's Paw.

Popular Colonel Donnelly served Choteau County as clerk, recorder and probate judge and was elected to the Twelfth Montana Territorial Legislature in 1881, being chosen Speaker of the House of Representatives. Throughout his time in Montana, Donnelly engaged in the practice of the law.

During 1883–84, when Louis Riel, leader of the Canadian Metis, was in exile in Montana, he spent time with Colonel Donnelly. According to writer Joseph Kinsey Howard, Donnelly offered his support and advice, advising Riel on the wording of petitions and military strategy. Donnelly told Riel that he considered Riel's dream of Metis freedom in western Canada a splendid one. Riel's 1885 invasion, defeat and hanging must have been a cruel blow to old Fenian Donnelly.

During 1885, Fort Benton was home for many Civil War veterans, and in early August of that year, Union veterans signed a petition to form a Grand Army of the Republic post. Among those signing this list was "J.J. Donnelly, Lt. Colonel, 14th Michigan."

Donnelly never remarried, and as he advanced in age, his memories of battles lost and won in the Civil War, the loss of his young wife, defeats in his Fenian cause, the defeat of the Metis and loss of Riel all must have weighed heavily on his mind. In November 1897, Donnelly was found lying in his bedroom with his throat badly cut, unconscious from loss of blood. Although he eventually recovered, the end was nearing for the old warrior, and his drinking increased.

Two years later, in September 1899, friends became concerned over his strange absence of several days. A search began, and footprints were discovered leading down to the edge of the Missouri River. When last seen, Donnelly had been drunk, and friends became concerned that the colonel had met with some mishap. For weeks the search continued, and a month later, remains were found on a sandbar on the south side of the Missouri River, having floated some sixty miles from the place where the tragedy occurred. Although badly decomposed, the body was identified as Donnelly's. The remains indicated a determined case of suicide as ruled by a coroner's jury.

After a special requiem Mass, the remains of Colonel Donnelly were interred in Riverside Cemetery by pallbearers including GAR veterans Thomas A. Cummings and Robert S. Culbertson. A large number of his old friends attended the simple ceremony.

Joseph Kinsey Howard, in *Strange Empire* eulogized Civil War veteran and Fenian leader Colonel Donnelly: "In September, 1899, the last of the Pembina plotters, last of the irreconcilables, perhaps last of the Fenian fighting men, joined his comrades. General Donnelly walked down to the Fort Benton levee, filled his pockets with fourteen pounds of rocks, slit his throat from ear to ear, and marched unfalteringly into the Missouri river." Colonel John J. Donnelly, Civil War hero, literally marched into history.

FORTUNES MADE AND FORTUNES LOST: CORPORAL WILLIAM SCOTT WETZEL

William Scott Wetzel served in the Civil War and came west to Montana Territory to make and lose fortunes.

Born in Pennsylvania on January 3, 1843, Scott Wetzel moved to Ohio with his family and later to Burlington, Iowa, where he enlisted in the 25th Iowa Infantry Regiment in August 1862. His regiment was assigned to the Army of Tennessee and participated in the siege of Vicksburg; the Battles of Lookout Mountain, Missionary Ridge, Kennesaw Mountain and Atlanta; and Sherman's March to the Sea. Scott Wetzel shared the experience at the Battle of Lookout Mountain with two other Union veterans in Montana: G.S. Vanderveer and Dave Fisher. All three proudly served in Fifteen Corps under Major General John A. Logan in that decisive Union victory on November 24, 1863. Wetzel was promoted to full corporal and served until his regiment was discharged in Washington, D.C., on June 6, 1865.

In 1866, Scott Wetzel arrived in Helena, Montana Territory, to engage in mining. Two years later, he moved on to Fort Benton and began to build a merchandising business. Joining forces with Joseph David Weatherwax in 1872, Wetzel & Weatherwax grew into a major trading firm, with most of its business focused on the bison robe trade with the Blackfoot Indians. J.D. Weatherwax had a murky past during the Civil War, making and losing a fortune as a cotton trader in New Orleans before coming up the Missouri

River in 1867 to Fort Benton, where he was elected sheriff in extensive Choteau County.

In the years before the arrival of the North West Mounted Police in 1874, Wetzel & Weatherwax joined other Fort Benton free traders in establishing trading posts in western Canada. For three years, the profits in this Canadian robe trade were substantial, until Weatherwax became one of the first Americans charged by the newly arrived North West Mounted Police with use of whiskey in the Indian trade. Weatherwax was fined, imprisoned for six months and lost several hundred impounded robes. Intimidated by this harsh treatment, Wetzel & Weatherwax moved its business south of the border.

William Scott Wetzel, Civil War veteran and Fort Benton free trader. *Overholser Historical Research Center.*

Weatherwax withdrew from the firm in 1880, while Scott Wetzel continued his profitable business, building a palatial mansion in Fort Benton in 1882. Two years later, Wetzel's firm failed, a victim of his extravagant spending and generosity in extending credit to all who asked. Wetzel's financial and physical health never fully recovered. He moved his family to the new town of Great Falls in 1887 and opened a real estate and brokerage firm.

At age forty-eight, Scott Wetzel passed away on April 20, 1891, leaving his mixed-race native Indian wife and three small children. His funeral services at Old Highland Cemetery were conducted by the Masonic Lodge, after which members of the GAR gathered around the grave. With bent heads, they solemnly listened to that sound so familiar in military life that marks the close of day—Taps. A young bugler stepped to the head of the grave and with his bugle blew Taps, and the mortal remains of Corporal William Scott Wetzel were consigned to the grave.

FROM THE CIVIL WAR TO LIBRARY FOUNDER: PRIVATE AUGUST WEDSWORTH[10]

When you walk down North Front Street in the small town of Cascade, stop at No. 13 to visit the Wedsworth Memorial Library. This lively little library honors Private Augustus Wedsworth, a Civil War soldier who enjoyed enormous success cattle ranching and became a benefactor for the Cascade community.

Born on October 1, 1842, in DuPage County, in northeastern Illinois, Augustus Wedsworth grew up on his family's farm. By the age of nine, he left school to work as a farmhand for three dollars per month plus room and board.

In the second year of the Civil War, the 100th Illinois Infantry was formed. On August 13, 1862, Augustus Wedsworth enlisted at Joliet, Illinois, in Company F for three years' service. The 100th Illinois proved an effective fighting force. During its first engagement near Bardstown, Kentucky, the regiment was ordered to conduct a charge, and charge it did, driving the Confederates out of town and two miles beyond. In the regiment's next engagement at Stone's River, Tennessee, while Union major general William S. Rosecrans's right flank was being routed, the 100th gallantly charged, forcing the Confederates to fall back. In a third bloody engagement three days later, the 100th assaulted a unit of Confederate lieutenant general John Bell Hood's Army of Tennessee and drove it back, causing heavy loss.

The 100th Illinois fought in key battles at Chickamauga, Georgia, and Lookout Mountain and Missionary Ridge, Tennessee, and in many engagements and skirmishes during the 120-day march from Chattanooga to Atlanta in 1864. Overall, the regiment suffered severe losses of 205 killed, died from disease or wounded. Private Wedsworth survived and served until the regiment was mustered out on June 12, 1865, at Nashville, Tennessee.

In 1866, Augustus Wedsworth came west to Montana Territory, finding work tending stock for A.J. Oliver's stage line between Helena and Virginia City. Saving his money, he purchased a wagon team and began freighting from Helena to mining camps. After Wedsworth mined for a short time, he bought 170 acres on Lepley Creek (northwest of Cascade) in 1875 and opened a dairy, selling products to the army at nearby Fort Shaw. Parlaying this success into $3,500 profit, in January 1884 he took up a 140-acre homestead

---

10. Earlier version published in *Tribune*, August 26, 2012.

Civil War veteran August Wedsworth's legacy led to the Wedsworth Memorial Library in the town of Cascade, Montana. *From Progressive Men of Montana.*

and began ranching in the Chestnut Valley. As a highly successful rancher, Wedsworth purchased other local ranches and expanded his operations.

In 1910, Augustus Wedsworth sold his ranching interests and moved to Cascade, residing there until his death on January 14, 1915. He was interred in Chestnut Valley Cemetery, although today he rests in Cascade's Hillside Cemetery. At the time of his death, he was president of Cascade Milling & Elevator Company, director of the First State Bank and vice-president of the Cascade Mercantile Company. Old soldier Wedsworth was an active member of Sheridan Post No. 18, GAR, in Great Falls.

Having no wife or children, Wedsworth's estate provided about $35,000 for family members. He left the bulk of his estate to the City of Cascade to erect a public library and gymnasium. Wedsworth's gift to his fellow citizens provided for Wedsworth Memorial Hall and Library. Wedsworth Hall was established in a building on South Front Street originally known as the Cascade Opera House. Built in 1908 by the Modern Woodmen of America Lodge, it was intended as a lodge room and recreation center. The effort was not a financial success, so it was taken over by local businessmen who formed the Cascade Opera Company.

In 1920, using Wedsworth Trust funds, the Cascade Opera House was enlarged, remodeled and renamed Wedsworth Memorial Hall. The formal opening of the hall occurred on the evening of October 1, 1921, with a large crowd attending a patriotic program. For many years, the young people of Cascade used Wedsworth Hall as a basketball court, while the community operated it as a recreation hall and theater. Since construction of a new school gymnasium, Wedsworth Hall has continued in use as a recreation center.

For some reason, the library portion of Wedsworth's dream came to Cascade much later. Cascade's first library opened in September 1936 in the basement of Stockman's Bank, moving the next year to Wedsworth Hall.

It remained there until 1976, when it was moved to its current location at 13 North Front Street. Today's Wedsworth Memorial Library, funded in part by the Wedsworth Trust, honors Civil War soldier Private Augustus Wedsworth, who, after serving his country, left an indelible mark on his community.

FROM "PAP" PRICE'S ARMY TO MONTANA TERRITORY: SERGEANT JOHN BYRD[11]

Confederate veterans fought and died for their cause, the War for Southern Independence. But in the state of Missouri, more than soldiers died, as the conflict became one of "total warfare," sweeping though the civilian population in farms and towns with an exceptional ferocity. For the Confederacy, the Missouri State Guard under General Sterling "Old Pap" Price conducted much of the fighting. Supporting the partisan rangers of the State Guard were quasi-military units such as William Clarke Quantrill's raiders and Bloody Bill Anderson's gang. These units, although under the Confederate army for much of the war, wrote their own rules of warfare and often dressed in civilian clothes or Union uniforms. They left a bloody trail as they employed hit-and-run tactics, often taking no prisoners.

As with many unconventional forces of the Confederacy, few records were kept or survive, and this is the case with John Byrd Sr., who died near Canyon Ferry, Montana, on February 28, 1905. Byrd was born in the Shenandoah Valley of Virginia in 1826. When he was ten years old, his family moved west to Liberty, Clay County, Missouri. He married Miss Emmeline Owens and settled into farming. After taking part in the Mexican War, Byrd joined the California gold rush in 1849. Mining for a short time, Byrd began freighting from Sonora to the mining camps. In 1853, he returned to Missouri by ship via the Isthmus of Panama.

According to his obituary, Byrd was a very prosperous farmer until the Civil War broke out: "He went to the war as a Confederate officer under General Price, and fought all through the war. When he returned home he had not much left. All his slaves were gone, all his horses were stolen and all other property in bad shape."

The 1890 U.S. Veterans Census intended for Union veterans and their widows inadvertently recorded Confederate veteran John Byrd living in

---

11. Earlier version published in *Tribune*, November 25, 2012.

New York Gulch, Meagher County: "John Byrd Sr., Sergeant, Company G, 4ᵗʰ Missouri State Guard enlisted September 16, 1861 discharged April 16, 1862, seven months service." This entry was annotated, "Conf." for Confederate and then crossed out. This offers strong evidence that John Byrd did serve in the Missouri State Guard.

A Byrd family oral history records, "Our family…tells this tale: John Byrd rode with Cantrell's [Quantrill's] raiders, so he was being hunted after the Civil War, by both sides. [His wife] Emmeline hid him in the fields on their plantation in Missouri, gave him money and provisions and wishing him a safe journey, sent him on

Confederate soldier Sergeant John Byrd, who served under General Sterling Price in Missouri, at his cabin in 1905 at Canyon Ferry, Montana. *Author's collection.*

his way to Montana alone, leaving her and their children behind."

Byrd's obituary records that he started for Colorado late in the fall of 1863 and wintered near Pike's Peak, hunting buffalo. The next spring, he stampeded to Alder Gulch, arriving on May 6, 1864. After mining for two years, Byrd moved on to New York Gulch on the Missouri River near Helena, mining there for several years. By 1870, the Byrd family was reunited in Montana, and John began cattle ranching, to continue until his death in 1905.

Culling available records, in 1860 John Byrd lived at Preston, Platte County, Missouri, with his family and just two female slaves, not the "large number of slaves" mentioned in his obituary.

A combination of the gold rush in Montana and the decisive defeat of General Price's army in 1964 brought many Missourians to the new territory during and after the Civil War, including Sergeant John Byrd. Today, Confederate John Byrd Sr. rests in the cemetery at Canyon Ferry, Montana.

Chapter 4

Black Americans

From Emancipation to the Firing Line

Although the Civil War began as an effort to reunify the Union after Southern secession, there were important underlying currents beyond that. For abolitionists and enslaved black Americans, the war meant far more than unification; rather, it was a struggle for freedom and equality. As the war lengthened and casualties mounted, President Lincoln moved to abolish slavery through a combination of emancipation and constitutional amendment. Facing political reality, his strategy became immediate freedom in the western territories, emancipation in the occupied South enforced by Union arms, toleration in the short term in the border states and a permanent solution through congressional amendment.

Colonel Robert Gould Shaw took command of the first black regiment raised in the North, the 54th Massachusetts Infantry. Montana carries this hero's name through the military post at Fort Shaw and today's small town. Two fighting men from the 54th Massachusetts came to Montana Territory after the war: Privates Joe Meek and Alexander Branson. Their stories tell much about the important role of black Americans in the Civil War. Young combat veterans Sergeant Charles Meek and U.S. Navy landsman William Morgan later played important roles in Montana Territory when Sergeant Meek became the first black juror in the territory and sailor Morgan became the first black elected to public office in the state. Both men acquired unusual stature within their community through their talent, Civil War service and membership in the GAR.

Also representing black Americans who came to Montana after the war, James Wesley Crump and Clarissa Jane Powell Crump met and married in

Montana and have descendants here today. Sergeant Crump served bravely in the war and was a leader in Helena's GAR, while his wife, Clarissa Jane, gained her freedom in the new Montana Territory.

FROM DEATH AND GLORY TO FORT SHAW: COLONEL ROBERT GOULD SHAW[12]

For four long years, our nation fought the most brutal and decisive war in our history—the American Civil War. One soldier who did not come to Montana was heroic Colonel Robert Gould Shaw, yet his name is still with us today. Colonel Shaw is the namesake for Fort Shaw in the Sun River Valley. In the late spring of 1867, the army constructed a military post in the valley to guard freight and passengers on the Benton-to-Helena road. The post first carried the name Camp Reynolds, according to Sun River historian Dick Thoroughman, to honor Major General John Reynolds, a hero in the first day of the Battle of Gettysburg. By August 1, 1867, the new military post was named Fort Shaw, and that name remained as the military post transitioned in 1892 into an Indian Industrial School and today's small town.

Born on October 19, 1837, Robert Gould Shaw was raised in a wealthy Massachusetts family immersed in the concept of *noblesse oblige* and active in the abolitionist movement. Harvard-educated Robert Shaw joined one of the first Northern regiments raised after the secession of several Southern states. His 7th New York Infantry Regiment marched to the defense of Washington, D.C., in April 1861. A month later, Second Lieutenant Shaw joined the 2nd Massachusetts Infantry, fighting in the battles of Winchester, Cedar Mountain and Antietam. His biographer, Russell Duncan, states that this "Blue-Eyed Child of Fortune" was merely a "competent" officer. Yet Robert Shaw was destined to rise to the threshold where death and glory meet.

President Abraham Lincoln issued the Emancipation Proclamation on January 1, 1863. Within weeks, two African American regiments were authorized in Massachusetts, the first black troops to be raised in the North. Colonel Robert Gould Shaw assumed command to organize and lead the 54th Massachusetts Infantry Regiment. Despite skeptics who argued, "Negroes will not fight," the new regiment formed and prepared for war. Colonel

---

12. Earlier version published in *Tribune*, September 25, 2012.

Left: Colonel Robert Gould Shaw, who led the 54th Massachusetts Infantry Regiment into death and glory at Fort Wagner, South Carolina. *Author's collection*.

Below: Chromolithograph by Kurz & Allison of the storming of Fort Wagner by the 54th Massachusetts Infantry, led by Colonel Robert Gould Shaw. *Library of Congress*.

Shaw, too, was dubious about his own free black unit, but the dedication of his men deeply impressed him, and he grew to respect them as fine soldiers.

On the afternoon of July 18, 1863, the men of the 54th Massachusetts spearheaded an assault on the Confederate stronghold of Fort Wagner on the approach to Charleston, South Carolina. Colonel Shaw died on a parapet, shouting, "Forward, 54th, forward!" as he led his men over the breastworks at Fort Wagner. The 54th Massachusetts fought bravely, suffering nearly 50 percent casualties (272 casualties in the 600-man force), and proved forever that black men could fight and die every bit the equal of whites.

Colonel Robert Shaw and his 54th Massachusetts achieved glory at heavy cost. Today, the town of Fort Shaw and Fort Shaw National Historic District proudly bear his name.

First Black American Warrior in the North: Private Alexander Branson[13]

Alexander Branson claimed to be the first black American to enlist in the North during the Civil War, and he might well have been. He was the first to enlist in the famed 54th Massachusetts Infantry Regiment, lived though the desperate assault at Fort Wagner, fought through other battles and skirmishes until the end of the war and came to the Montana frontier to settle in Lewistown, Montana, in the 1880s. Alex Branson lived over forty years in the Judith Basin, earning the respect of his fellow veterans and the affection of his community, where he was known as "Uncle Alex."

Born in 1840 in the slave-owning society of Charleston, Virginia (today's West Virginia), Alex Branson likely was born into slavery. He was free before the beginning of the Civil War, although how he attained his freedom is not known. By 1860, he had made his way to Philadelphia, where he worked as a barber.

In early 1863, Governor John A. Andrew, war governor of Massachusetts and a passionate opponent of slavery, obtained permission from President Lincoln to recruit a regiment of "colored" men in his state. Only three colored regiments had been formed prior to that time: Brigadier General Rufus Saxton recruited the 1st South Carolina Volunteers (Union) in August 1862 from contrabands (escaped slaves freed in the South by Union forces);

---

13. Earlier version published in *River Press*, April 25, May 2, 2012.

Major General Benjamin F. Butler organized the 1st Louisiana Native Guards (Union) from free blacks in September 1862; and Colonel James M. Williams mustered in the 1st Kansas Infantry (Colored) in January 1863.

The 54th Massachusetts Infantry Regiment was the first military unit composed of men of African descent raised in the North. Companies were mustered in between March 30 and May 13, with the recruits coming from all parts of Massachusetts as well as other states. Since more enlistments were secured than were needed, the surplus became the nucleus of a second regiment, the 55th Massachusetts.

When Governor Andrew received his orders from Secretary of War Edwin M. Stanton, he at once appointed Captain Robert Gould Shaw as colonel and Captain Norwood P. Hallowell as lieutenant colonel. Both men accepted but were on duty in the South at the time. Captain Hallowell was the first to start north to begin organizing the new regiment. He stopped at Philadelphia to visit relatives for a few days and, while there, recruited a number of men for the new regiment. Alexander Branson was one of eight men enlisted by Captain Hallowell on February 18, his first day of recruiting, and Branson claimed to be the first in line to sign on for the three-year term as private. Since no recruiting had yet been started in Boston, these eight men were the first recruits of the 54th Massachusetts. Samuel Branson, a Philadelphia shoemaker and likely related to Alexander, was also among these recruits.

So great was the sentiment in the North against allowing black Americans to take up arms that Captain Hallowell was compelled to slip his recruits out of Philadelphia by stealth, and the Bransons were in the first group to be sent to Boston. Upon reaching there, the recruits mustered in, and on March 30, Alexander and Samuel Branson were assigned to Company B under Captain Robert R. Newell. All commissioned officers of the regiment were white men as the regiment began training.

Leaving camp on May 28, the 54th Massachusetts, led by Colonel Shaw and with Private Alexander Branson proudly carrying his new Enfield rifle, passed in review by Governor Andrew on Boston Common before the largest crowd in Boston history. The regiment embarked on the transport ship *DeMolay* the same day bound for combat duty along the coast of South Carolina. On July 8, the regiment proceeded to Stono Inlet, where it became part of General Alfred Terry's expedition to James Island near Charleston. Near Secessionville on July 16, the Union forces were attacked by a Confederate brigade under Brigadier General Alfred H. Colquitt, and in the battle that followed, the 54th suffered thirty-five casualties. The 54th had come successfully through its first combat action.

Monument on Boston Common with Colonel Shaw leading his 54th Massachusetts, the first African American regiment raised in the North. *Library of Congress.*

Ordered to report to Brigadier General George C. Strong on Morris Island, on July 18, the 54th Massachusetts was chosen to lead an assault on Fort Wagner, a strategic bastion protecting Charleston. Colonel Shaw deployed his 624 men in two wings, five companies on the left and five on the right, with Company B on the right flank of the right wing. At 7:45 p.m., Shaw raised his sword and addressed his men: "Move in quick time until within a hundred yards of the fort; then double quick and charge!...Forward!" The 54th Massachusetts advanced down the beach and into history.

The assault of the 54th Massachusetts Infantry on Fort Wagner became legend. Its brigade commander, General Strong, reported, "Under cover of darkness [the 54th] stormed the fort, faced a stream of fire, faltered not till the ranks were broken by shot and shell; and in all these severe tests, which would have tried even veteran troops, they fully met my expectations, for many were killed, wounded, or captured on the walls of the fort." The 54th suffered 272 casualties, yet the troops' bravery under withering fire was acclaimed throughout the North. Among the casualties were Colonel Robert Gould

Shaw; 2 captains and about 133 men killed or missing; Lieutenant Colonel Edward N. Hallowell (who earlier had replaced his brother Norwood); 10 commissioned officers; and 125 men wounded. Despite the staggering losses, Private Alex Branson and the 54th proved to both North and South that black troops would fight and fight effectively.

All through the month of August, the regiment constructed entrenchments and parallels, gradually pushing closer to Fort Wagner and forcing evacuation by Confederates forces on September 7. The 54th Massachusetts was given the honor of leading entry of the earthworks and occupation of Fort Wagner.

The autumn of 1863 was spent in the reconstruction of Forts Wagner and Gregg so that they would face toward Fort Sumter and Charleston and in erecting other fortifications. By October 17, Lieutenant Colonel E.N. Hallowell had overcome his wounds and, promoted to colonel, returned to assume command of the 54th. In January 1864, the 54th was assigned to an expedition along the Florida coast commanded by Major General Truman Seymour. The 54th moved into the interior and, on February 20, engaged the enemy near Olustee while covering the retirement of General Seymour's force from that place, suffering eighty-seven casualties. Olustee was the largest battle fought in Florida during the Civil War.

The 54th returned to Morris Island in April and spent the summer and fall of 1864 in the fortifications on James and Morris Islands. The regiment conducted small-scale operations until May 6, when most of the regiment was distributed around occupied South Carolina. District headquarters detailed Private Branson as an orderly in a mayor's office. Branson and his regiment reassembled at Mount Pleasant on August 17 to embark on the transports *C.F. Thomas* and *Ashland*. The 54th reached Boston Harbor on August 27–28 and five days later was reviewed by the governor, paraded through Boston Common and Beacon Hill and then disbanded. Private Alex Branson received $38.89 pay and a bounty of $100.

An important chapter in the history of the 54th was its fight for regular soldier's pay of thirteen dollars per month. At the outset, Governor Andrew had assured the men that they would receive the same pay as all other volunteer soldiers. But in July 1863, an order came from Washington fixing the compensation of colored soldiers at ten dollars per month. Several times this offer was made to the men of the 54th, but each time they declined. Refusing their reduced pay became a point of honor for the men of the 54th.

In November 1863, the legislature of Massachusetts passed an act providing that the difference of three dollars per month should be made up by the state, but the men of the regiment refused to accept this money.

They demanded that they receive their full soldier pay from the Federal government. For eighteen months after first entering service, the men received nothing for their service and suffering. Finally, in September 1864, the Federal government met their demand, and all members of the regiment received full pay from the time of their enlistment.

The 54th Massachusetts Regiment was widely acclaimed for its valor during the Battle of Fort Wagner. The troops' actions proved that black men would fight and die in defense of their country. Their valor helped encourage the further enlistment and mobilization of about 300,000 black troops, a key development that President Abraham Lincoln once noted as helping to secure the final victory. The legacy of the 54th Massachusetts since the Civil War has been remarkable. In 1867, the new fort in the Sun River Valley in Montana Territory was named Fort Shaw as a tribute to Colonel Robert Gould Shaw. A monument to the 54th, constructed by Augustus Saint-Gaudens on Boston Common, is part of the Boston Black Heritage Trail. A famous composition by Charles Ives, "Col. Shaw and His Colored Regiment," the opening movement of *Three Places in New England (Orchestral Set No. 1)*, is based on the 54th. Colonel Shaw and his men also feature prominently in Robert Lowell's Civil War Centennial poem "For the Union Dead" (1964). Most recently, the movie *Glory* won the 1989 Academy Award for best picture and reestablished the now-popular image of the role African Americans played in the Civil War.

Private Alexander Branson survived Fort Wagner and the other skirmishes and battles to the end of the Civil War. After his discharge on August 20, 1865, he returned to Philadelphia and worked there during the 1870s as a barber. Little is known of his life during this period, but he probably joined with his fellow veterans, black and white, in the GAR. By 1880, he was on his way west, living in Sioux City, Iowa, where he worked as a barber.

Alex Branson continued up the Missouri River to Fort Benton by steamboat in 1881 and settled in the Judith Basin. By this time, the bison herds had been reduced and cattle ranching was taking over the Judith, and Branson engaged in stock raising. As the town of Lewistown began to grow after 1883, he moved there and started a barbershop.

Branson filed claim for a 160-acre homestead in July 1887 on the west fork of Beaver Creek southwest of Lewistown. The 1890 U.S. Census Veterans Schedule recorded twenty-six Union veterans living in Lewistown, with Private "Elick" Branson, Company B, 54th Massachusetts Regiment, listed first. After a fire destroyed his barbershop, Branson built a replacement frame building. Advertisements ran in the *Fergus County Argus* for this new shop, "Gem Shaving

Private Alexander Branson, 54th Massachusetts and member of the GAR (rear right), with the Reed family at his home in Lewistown, Montana. *Art Ball Collection.*

Parlors Alexander Branson, Proprietor Main Street, Lewistown, Montana Best appointed shop in eastern Montana." On New Year's Eve 1891, when the James A. Shields Post No. 19 of the GAR met to select new officers, Alex Branson was named surgeon, one of fifteen to hold office. Throughout his years in Lewistown, Branson remained active in the GAR.

The next year, the Republican Party of Lewistown organized a Lincoln Club with Alex Branson among its members. Later that year, he completed proving up his homestead and received patent to the land. He owned other land in the same area, operating a ranch at the head of Little Rock Creek.

Active in ranching, business and politics, Alexander Branson gained the respect of the Lewistown community. In May 1894, with three other GAR members, he arranged Memorial Day activities.

Although his Civil War service record reported no battle wounds, Branson suffered early from rheumatism, and in July 1896, he was granted a Civil War invalid pension, which was renewed in 1903.

In 1898, Branson partnered with Mr. Danioth to operate the Occidental Restaurant in Lewistown. The following year, when Lewistown held a grand reception to welcome home soldiers from the Spanish-American War, Branson was the veterans' color-bearer in the Line of March into the city. In 1900, Alex served as a trial juror in the district court, making him one of the early blacks to serve on a jury in Montana.

Alexander Branson left Lewistown in late September 1902 for Washington, D.C., to attend the Thirty-sixth GAR National. Encampment at Camp Roosevelt on October 9–10 in the shadow of the Washington Monument. The *Argus* reported:

> *Alex. Branson is a well-known citizen of Lewistown and is one of the G.A.R. veterans left in this section of the state. He served during the war with the 54th Mass. Regiment in the capacity of color bearer. The regiment did excellent service and was the first colored regiment recruited in the north. It was under the command of Col. Shaw, after whom old Fort Shaw was named.*

Over the next two decades, Alex Branson remained active, although he was slowed by age and ailments and eventually had to retire at age eighty. He lived comfortably with the property he had accumulated and his invalid pension from the government. His great desire was to attend the National Encampment of the GAR in Boston in 1924 to see one last time Boston Common, where he had paraded with his regiment on their way to war nearly sixty years before. Unfortunately, during the winter of 1923–24, his rheumatism reached a stage where he was unable to care for himself.

"Uncle Alex" Branson left Lewistown in the fall of 1924 to spend his remaining days with a niece, Mrs. Roy Hamit, in Pittsburgh. Lewistown lost a resident respected by the entire community, and Montana lost an honored Civil War veteran, when Alexander Branson passed away in Philadelphia at age ninety-four on December 26, 1934. Today, Private Alexander Branson rests in Philadelphia National Cemetery.

FROM THE EMBANKMENTS OF FORT WAGNER TO THE BARKER MINES: PRIVATE JOSEPH W. MEEK[14]

Gravestone of Private Joseph W. Meek, Company E, 54th Massachusetts Infantry Regiment, at Mayn Cemetery, White Sulphur Springs, Montana. *Author's collection.*

When Colonel Robert Gould Shaw and his 54th Massachusetts Infantry Regiment paraded through Boston Common on their way to war, Private Joseph Meek marched in their ranks. Today, Private Meek rests in Mayn Cemetery, White Sulphur Springs, after a life of adventure during the Civil War and later in the mountains of Montana.

Joseph W. Meek was born in 1843, son of Solomon and Amanda Maria Meek, slaves on a plantation in Tennessee. In the 1850s, Joseph and his younger brother Charles either escaped or were freed and made their way northward. By 1858, Joseph Meek and his wife, Laura, were living in Illinois, where their son Henry was born that year.

When the Emancipation Proclamation was issued, Joseph Meek, age twenty, worked as a shoemaker in Springfield, Ohio. Like many young blacks, Meek anxiously awaited the opportunity to join the Union army. On May 12, 1863, he enlisted for three years at Readville, Massachusetts, in Company E, 54th Massachusetts. Two weeks later, on May 28, with Privates Meek and Alexander Branson in the ranks, Colonel Shaw led the 54th Massachusetts through the streets of Boston to board the transport ship *DeMolay*, bound for duty in South Carolina.

Private Joseph Meek participated in the same action in South Carolina with the 54th as had Private Branson, including the assault on Fort Wagner. Private Meek and the other survivors went on to further action in South Carolina and Florida. They took part in battles at Olustee, Honey Hill and

---

14. Earlier version published in *Tribune*, October 30, 2011.

Boykin Hill. Private Joseph Meek mustered every month throughout the war until his discharge on August 20, 1865.

After the war, Joseph and Laura Meek and son Henry moved to Kansas City, Missouri. In the late 1870s, Joe Meek left his family with his parents in Kansas and embarked a steamboat to go up the Missouri River to Fort Benton. Settling in the Little Belt Mountains, in 1880 Meek worked as a shoemaker. That fall, with friend Samuel Spaulding, Meek began prospecting at the Barker Mines, where the *Benton Record* reported the "two lucky prospectors" returned to Fort Benton with samples of ore taken from a new lode, named "Laura" for Joseph's wife.

One year later, while hunting on Old Baldy Mountain, Joe Meek discovered a ledge of silver ore up in a region of perpetual snow. With help from friends, Meek drove off claim jumpers and opened the Meek lode, packing ore down the mountain two miles on a mule for the smelter at Barker. With his mining success, Meek brought his wife and son to Barker.

After years of profitable small-scale mining, Joe Meek and his family moved to White Sulphur Springs. He continued prospecting and mining while his wife served as nurse and midwife assisting Drs. Kumpe and MacKay. The Meek home was located along a hill just northeast of the famed Castle at White Sulphur Spring.

Joseph W. Meek, a respected member of the White Sulphur Springs community, died on August 27, 1912, and was interred in Lot 28 at Mayn Cemetery. His grave marker proudly bears the inscription honoring his Civil War service: "Jos. W. Meek Co. E. 54 Mass. Inf."

FROM TEENAGE SERGEANT TO POLITICAL LEADER: TRAILBLAZER CHARLES M. MEEK[15]

Born a slave with his brother Joseph on a Tennessee plantation in January 1849, Charles M. Meek attained a record of achievement and adventure. He spent his early boyhood days as a servant in his master's house. When the Civil War began, Charles Meek either escaped or was freed from bondage and fell in with Union troops, becoming a personal servant on the staff of General Ulysses Grant. Young Charles Meek was illiterate, but an officer on Grant's staff became interested in the boy and taught him to read and write.

---

15. Earlier version published in *Tribune*, February 26, 2012.

Meek learned so quickly that before leaving Grant's service, the general offered to send him to college. Meek declined, and when Grant went to the Eastern Theater to become commanding general in March 1864, Meek remained in Kentucky.

In September 1864, fifteen-year-old Charles Meek reported his age as eighteen to join Company D, 5th Cavalry Regiment, U.S. Colored Troops, at Lebanon, Kentucky. Under regimental commander Colonel James Brisbin, a prominent abolitionist, the 5th U.S. Colored Cavalry (USCC), former slaves with white officers, participated in Burbridge's Raid into southwestern Virginia during September–October 1864, when they saw fierce action at Saltville, Virginia. In the later Stoneman's Raid during December, the 5th USCC participated in the capture of Saltville and destruction of an important Confederate saltworks.

Despite his age, Meek proved a natural leader and was promoted to corporal on May 1, 1865, and sergeant just two months later. The 5th USCC was stationed in Arkansas after the war hunting down Rebel renegades, supervising free elections and trying to protect officeholders and freedmen from counter-Reconstruction violence. Sergeant Meek left the army in January 1866, married and settled at Prairie, near Kansas City, Kansas.

In 1880, Charles Meek came up the Missouri River to Fort Benton to join his older brother Joseph and seek his fortune in the Barker Mines in the Little Belt Mountains. Charles developed mining claims in Barker and nearby Yogo but lacked the capital to develop them. He settled in the new town of Great Falls in 1887 and the next year, in November, was selected as juror in district court, the first known black juror in Montana. Charles Meek became active in the African Methodist Episcopal (AME) Church, the GAR and Republican Party politics and organized a Colored Lincoln Republican Club. From 1889 to 1894, Meek was elected delegate to Cascade County Republican conventions. In the 1894 convention, he gave an eloquent speech that triggered the nomination of William Morgan for Great Falls townsite constable, the first black man to be nominated and elected to public office in Montana. In March 1891, Meek served a second time as juror in Cascade County and in 1895 served as juror in the Crowe murder trial.

In the fall of 1895, Meek returned to Kansas, and the *Tribune* observed, "Mr. Meek has...won for himself the respect of the community...the colored people of Great Falls will lose one of their brightest representatives and a natural leader, and Great Falls will lose a patriotic and worthy citizen." Ever the adventurer, eighteen months later he returned to Great Falls, but the lure of gold soon attracted him to the Klondike gold stampede, with the *Tribune* reporting, "Charlie Meek has been in the van of the pioneers all his life and he is confident that he will win fortune in Alaska."

Meek wrote insightful letters to the *Tribune* about the many failures and few successes in the "land of ice and gold." His letters advised that he "found the yellow metal everywhere, [but] failed to find it in paying quantities," with "only one or two in a hundred" finding paying claims. He observed, "Corruption reigns supreme in Dawson and the Klondike," yet he spoke "in terms of admiration of the grit and endurance displayed by the gold seekers."

After eighteen months, Meek returned from Alaska but soon moved on to mine in Idaho and Washington. In April 1901, he returned to Great Falls after being badly injured in a mining

Gravestone of Sergeant Charles M. Meek, 5th Kentucky Cavalry (Colored), Soldiers Plot, Highland Cemetery, Great Falls, Montana. *Author's collection.*

accident. The adventurous black pioneer died at Deaconess Hospital on April 6, 1910. Attended by brother Joseph and other GAR members, Sergeant Charles M. Meek was buried in Soldiers Plot, Highland Cemetery.

UNION SAILOR TO ELECTED GREAT FALLS CONSTABLE: LANDSMAN WILLIAM M. MORGAN[16]

In the election of November 1894, Great Falls elected an African American to public office—a first for the state of Montana. Civil War Union navy veteran William M. Morgan was elected Great Falls townsite constable.

---

16. Earlier version published in *Tribune*, September 30, 2012.

Born in Harrodsburg, Mercer County, Kentucky, on July 3, 1843, William Morgan was likely one of the 256 free blacks in that county. At the beginning of the Civil War, Morgan joined the Union navy and served as a landsman on the USS *Sabine* throughout the war. As a landsman, the rank given to new recruits in the navy, Morgan performed menial, unskilled work.

The history of the Civil War has been written largely about the armies and land battles on both sides. Yet historian James M. McPherson believes that "the Union navy deserves more credit for Northern victory than it has traditionally received." In August 1863, President Lincoln paid tribute to the Union navy in opening the Mississippi River and other Union naval successes.

William Morgan was one of about twenty thousand black Americans who served in the Union navy during the Civil War. This constituted an estimated 16 percent of the navy's enlisted force. The navy used integrated crews, with blacks working side by side with whites.

The USS *Sabine* was among the first ships to see action in the Civil War. A Brandywine-class frigate the *Sabine* was a 202-foot sailing ship carrying about fifty guns and a complement of four hundred officers and men. During the war, *Sabine* was actively deployed along the East Coast searching for Confederate commerce raiders. It participated in the relief and reinforcement of Fort Pickens, Florida, in April 1861; the rescue of three hundred marines and crew of chartered troop transport *Governor* with the loss of just seven during a violent storm off South Carolina on November 2–3, 1861; the search for USS *Vermont* in March 1862, after that ship-of-the-line had been badly damaged by a storm while sailing to Port Royal, South Carolina; and the hunt for successful commerce raiders CSS *Alabama* in October 1862 and CSS *Tacony* in June 1863. *Sabine* returned to New York for blockade duty with the North Atlantic Blockading Squadron until ordered in August 1864 to Norfolk, Virginia, as a training ship for navy apprentices and landsmen.

In 1882, William Morgan came up the Missouri River on the steamboat *Butte*, arriving at Fort Benton on May 7. After a short time working in that town, Owen H. Churchill hired Morgan to work on his large ranch in Sun River Valley. Morgan began homesteading in 1886 five miles south of Great Falls along the Missouri River, and he received patent to 158 acres five years later. As Great Falls began to grow, Morgan built a house on the lower Southside and became active in the black community, serving as a founding trustee in building an African Methodist Episcopal Church in 1891. He helped form Sunset Lodge #14, a black Masonic Lodge; and a black Odd Fellows Lodge.

Active in Republican Party politics, William Morgan was appointed to a plumb political job as janitor of the Cascade County Courthouse. In the election of 1894, he was nominated at the Republican convention with white candidate Joseph E. Huston for two positions as Great Falls townsite constable. On the night of November 6, 1894, Morgan went to bed after working that day as janitor at the courthouse. He awoke the next morning to learn that he'd received 503 votes to defeat the leading Democratic Party candidate by 24 votes and win election as constable. This marked the first election of a black American to public office in Montana.

After serving effectively in office from 1895 to 1897, Constable Morgan returned to his ranch, which had expanded by then to six hundred acres. He ranched and drove the Great Falls–to–Millegan

Gravestones of Landsman William M. Morgan, U.S. Navy, Old Highland Cemetery, Great Falls, Montana. *Author's collection.*

stagecoach. On March 24, 1899, Civil War Union navy veteran and constable William M. Morgan died at his home in Great Falls. The *Tribune* marked his passing with the headline "Death of a Good Citizen" and reported, "Exposure in this line of duty [driving the stage] aggravated an old injury and caused his death. He was an honest and industrious man, who commanded the respect and confidence of all who knew him." Landsman William Morgan rests in Old Highland Cemetery.

FREE BLACK AND SLAVE COME TO MONTANA TERRITORY: JAMES WESLEY AND CLARISSA JANE CRUMP[17]

From the first days of the Civil War, Missouri was torn between loyal Union and pro-secession elements. Slave owners and their slaves populated Little

---

17. Earlier version published in *Tribune,* January 27, 2013.

Dixie along the Missouri River corridor through the center of the state. Two African Americans from Little Dixie, James Wesley Crump and Clarissa Jane Powell, lived through the violent days of Civil War Missouri, migrated separately to Montana Territory and left descendants to tell their story.

James Wesley Crump was born a free black in 1847 in Jackson County, Missouri, near Kansas City. On July 15, 1864, at Leavenworth, Kansas, seventeen-year-old Crump enlisted as a private in the Douglas Independent Battery, U.S. Colored Light Artillery Brigade. With few exceptions, white officers commanded black units in the Civil War. Private Crump's battery, known as the Independent Colored Kansas Battery, was one of the exceptions—black officers led it. One of these black officers, Second Lieutenant William D. Matthews, enlisted Crump and his brother John into the Union army. In October 1864, the Kansas Battery entered combat just as Confederate major general Sterling Price began to invade Kansas from his base in Arkansas. The Kansas Battery went into action with two modern rifled Parrott 3-inch cannons manned by forty men. As part of the Third Brigade, the Kansas Battery joined other artillery units gaining praise from brigade commander Major General Samuel Curtis, who reported, "The enemy was soon overpowered...Every piece of artillery, especially the little howitzers, was active in fire, showing artillery enough to represent an army of 50,000."

The Kansas Battery then joined a weeklong running cavalry battle driving Price's army out of Kansas. In January 1865, Crump was promoted to corporal and served until July 22, 1865, when he was mustered out at Fort Leavenworth.

Clarissa Jane "Jennie" Powell was born a slave on August 2, 1854, and as the Civil War began, she lived with two other female slaves in the household of farmer Philip E. Evans in Pettis County, Missouri. Young Clarissa, still a slave, accompanied the Evans family when they boarded the steamboat *Lillie Martin* at St. Louis in April 1865 bound for the upper Missouri. These were turbulent times in Montana Territory, so at Fort Union, a "Guard of Soldiers" boarded to provide protection from native Indian harassment. The steamer struggled against low water in the river to arrive in late June at the mouth of the Marias River, where the passengers proceeded the twelve miles on to Fort Benton and Helena by wagon.

Clarissa was freed legally by her arrival in a western territory, before enactment of the Thirteenth Amendment to the Constitution in December 1865. She was educated by the Evans family and for the rest of her life remained in touch with the family, including their son, John Morgan Evans, who served as U.S. congressman from Montana.

Right: Mrs. Clarissa Jane Powell Crump, who came to Helena, Montana, as a slave in 1865 and was freed by passage of the Thirteenth Amendment. *Raymond Crump Howard Collection.*

Below: Corporal James Wesley Crump (center) holding a U.S. flag with the GAR at the dedication of the Montana State Capitol in Helena, July 4, 1902. *Raymond Crump Howard Collection.*

James Crump began freighting westward after the war and by 1869 was working for the Diamond R Freighting Company in Montana Territory, hauling freight to Helena and Fort Benton from Corrine, Utah, on the Union Pacific Railroad. In October 1869, James Crump married Clarissa Jane Powell at Corrine. After more than a decade of freighting and mining in the Butte and Marysville areas, the Crumps settled in Helena, where in 1885 James contracted for construction of their family home at 1003 Ninth Avenue. This longtime Crump home is on the National Register of Historic Places.

The Crumps were leaders of the Helena black community, including the St. James African Methodist Episcopal Church, Pleasant Hour Ladies Club, Manhattan Club, black Masonic and Odd Fellows Lodges and the GAR. They raised two daughters, Emma and Clarinda, and descendants remain in Montana, including Raymond Crump Howard and his wife, Charlene Nava, who have shared their family history and photographs, making this account possible.

James Wesley Crump, a strong and successful Montana pioneer, died on April 18, 1919. Clarissa Jane Powell Crump, described as "a woman of charm and character" and "the last black pioneer of the state," passed on March 10, 1941. Both pioneers rest today in Forestvale Cemetery, Helena.

In a tribute to the black soldiers who served in the Civil war, poet Paul Laurence Dunbar penned:

The Colored Soldiers
And their deeds shall find a record,
In the registry of fame;
For their blood has cleansed completely
Every blot of slavery's shame.
So all honor and all glory
To these noble Sons of Ham—
To the gallant colored soldiers,
Who fought for Uncle Sam!

Chapter 5

Children, Women, Men, Families

In Total War

During the course of its four years, the Civil War became a "total war" in the battleground states. Battle lines blurred with the ebb and flow of the fighting as ground was taken and retaken by both sides. The Civil War engaged communities and families in many ways. Teenage boys often exaggerated their age to enlist, while other youngsters found that they were on the battlefield as the fighting swirled around their towns and farms. Women held farms and families together but in many instances became active participants in various ways as nurse, spy, combatant, teacher and other roles. The young and the old in many areas simply were not "behind" the lines as the fighting closed in on them.

Representing this era of total war are several "veterans" who came to Montana after the war, such as teenage Will Van Orsdel, who by chance and geography became an active participant in the Battle of Gettysburg. Miss Harriet Lewis was recruited by the Freedmen's Bureau to go into the Deep South to teach freed slaves. A family team of Colonel and Mrs. Francis Malone represent the many families with fighting men accompanied by daring wives who came along as combat nurses. Miss Sarah Maranda Strong served in the small but emerging Union Nursing Corps. Miss Rebecca Norton helped the Union cause as a spy reporting important information to military commanders.

GROOMED ON THE BATTLEFIELD AT GETTYSBURG: YOUNG BROTHER VAN[18]

In the Civil War, men fought, women held families and homes together—and children were caught in between. All were profoundly affected by the war. Some teenage boys from both North and South enlisted at very young ages. Those who didn't, such as young William Wesley Van Orsdel, carried vivid memories of the war for the rest of their lives.

Will, the son of William and Mary (Osborn) Van Orsdel, was born on March 20, 1848, near Gettysburg, Pennsylvania. The youngest of seven children, young Will attended local schools and Hunterstown Academy. He joined the Methodist Church at the age of twelve.

On the first day of the Battle of Gettysburg, July 1, 1863, Confederate cavalry brigade commander Brigadier General Albert G. Jenkins, at his post on a sheltered hillside, told a rough-clad barefoot boy from a nearby farmhouse, "Now, boy, watch and you'll see one of the sights of the war! Our troops are going to charge and take that battery." That fifteen-year-old farm boy was Will Van Orsdel.

All through the first day, Van Orsdel watched the ebb and flow on the battlefield as the Confederates pushed the Federals back. Yet at the end of the day, Union forces under Brigadier General Oliver O. Howard held the high ground on Cemetery Ridge. Ignoring the danger all through the day, Will hurried from point to point, carrying water and cheer to the wounded on both sides in the midst of the greatest artillery engagement of the war.

Union reinforcements arrived during the night, and on the second day, Van Orsdel was back on the field helping in every way he could. Throughout the day, Confederate forces tried to take both Cemetery Ridge and Little Round Top without success, despite bloody losses. The action culminated on the third day with Pickett-Pettigrew-Trimble's Charge into the center of the Union line. This final assault failed with heavy casualties, and with that, General Robert E. Lee ordered his forces to withdraw, ending the great Battle of Gettysburg, the last Confederate invasion of the North.

Four months later, Will Van Orsdel was present when President Abraham Lincoln came to Gettysburg to deliver an address on November 19. After the speech, Will shook the president's hand.

The Battle of Gettysburg and the Gettysburg Address left profound impressions on young Will Van Orsdel. He dedicated his life to helping

---

18. Earlier version published in *Tribune*, June 30, 2013.

others and often gave lectures entitled "What a Boy Saw and Heard at the Battle of Gettysburg," relating his personal observations and impressions of the great battle.

Following the Civil War, Van Orsdel began missionary work in the oil fields of Pennsylvania, where he remained until March 1872. Then, boarding the steamboat *Far West*, he came up the Missouri River to Fort Benton, arriving on a rainy Sunday, June 30, 1872. Legend has it that "Brother Van," as he was nicknamed that first day, held his first prayer meeting in a saloon with the bar temporarily closed.

Cartoon by Harry W. Lytle featuring beloved Methodist circuit rider Reverend W.W. Van Orsdel "Brother Van." *From the* Great Falls Leader, *May 16, 1913.*

The next year, Brother Van received his first appointment, serving under Reverend Francis A. Riggin as a circuit-riding minister for Beaverhead and Jefferson Counties. From 1890, he served variously as presiding elder in Great Falls and Helena and as superintendent for the North Montana Mission, Great Falls and Milk River districts.

Brother Van went on to become one of the most loved men in Montana history. For almost fifty years, he rode the circuit and administered the North Montana Mission and the Montana Methodist Conference. During this time, he founded more than one hundred churches, a university, six hospitals and a children's home. He was inducted into the 2011 Montana Cowboy Hall of Fame with these words: "His charismatic, never-say-die faith drew to him people from every walk of life including Indians, and everyone from gunslingers to governors."

Brother Van was groomed on the battlefield at Gettysburg and served the people of Montana well. He died on December 19, 1919, and was interred in Forestvale Cemetery in Helena. Each Christmas, Brother Van sent cards to his many friends. In his last year, he had arranged for his 1919 Christmas cards to be sent out with the message "My first Christmas in Heaven." In recognition of his life of service and the impact he had on the people of Montana, the state and national flags at the capitol in Helena were lowered to half-mast. This rare honor for a private citizen was a tribute to beloved Brother Van, who sang, preached and prayed his way into the hearts of Montanans. As we commemorate the 150th anniversary of the Battle of Gettysburg, let our thoughts envision a young man serving the wounded on those hallowed grounds.

TEACHING FORMER SLAVES FOR THE FREEDMEN'S BUREAU: HARRIET A. LEWIS[19]

On Memorial Day 1897 at the Opera House in Great Falls, attorney William H. Smith paid moving tribute to the women of the Civil War:

Let us not forget the noble women of the war. Of their deeds of mercy and of heroism we seldom hear a word. And yet the preservation of this nation is largely due to their great patriotism and devotion...For four long years

---

19. Earlier version published in *Tribune*, October 28, 2012.

*mothers, wives, sisters and daughters worked and wept in that awful night
of grief. They nursed the sick, dressed the painful wounds and lulled the
parting souls to eternal peace.*

Women served many roles in the war beyond guarding desolate firesides
in their homes. Some served as nurses, some as spies, a few fought alongside
their male comrades in arms and others brought aid and knowledge to freed
slaves under the Freedmen's Bureau. Among the latter was young Harriet A.
Lewis, who led a most remarkable life.

Harriet Lewis was born in 1845, the daughter of Dr. William Lewis,
assigned by the American Missionary Society to a station in the wilderness
of western Lake Superior among the Chippewa Indians. At age fifteen,
Harriet was sent to her mother's former home at Tallmadge, Ohio, where
she attended Tallmadge Academy and graduated from Oberlin College.

In the last year of the Civil war, Harriet Lewis taught in the Freedmen's
schools in the South—not an easy occupation by any means, as those engaged
in this service were ostracized by local white Southerners. The Freedmen's
Bureau was a Federal agency that aided freed slaves in the South in the early

Harriet A. Lewis taught in a freedmen's school such as this one. *From Frank Leslie's Illustrated
Newspaper, November 17, 1866.*

years of Reconstruction. The bureau joined with benevolent societies to send over 1,300 teachers to the South in 1866. Of that number, about 220 were Northern white men and women. The teachers received an average salary of twenty to fifty dollars per month and took on responsibilities outside the classroom, often acting as missionaries, social workers, dispensers of charity, labor superintendents and legal advisers.

From 1865 to 1867, Harriet Lewis taught schools for freed slaves in the South. A glimpse into her experiences and challenges is found in two letters she wrote in 1866 while serving in Mississippi. Teaching in Aberdeen, Harriet noted that she was greeted locally as "nigger teacher Yank," though less often than she had been previously. She observed:

> *I find the Freedman here much oppressed and very destitute. I have visited among them all I could out of school hours, and in enough wretchedness and suffering to make the stoutest heart ache. I almost feel sometimes, as though it was wrong for us to be so very comfortable while there are so many poor, half clad, half starved creatures in the world, and I am thankful that I can do even a little to help them.*

In December 1866, Harriet transferred to a school in Brookhaven, in southern Mississippi. Living in a house with another teacher, she expressed concern for the environment surrounding them, writing, "If we can only keep our little house, but they are trying to turn us out of that. The house is rented of a Dutchman who lives next door, and he says that the white folks have threatened to burn it if we do not move out." Noting that she had "already given away everything of my own that I could spare," Harriet begged her cousin to send boxes of suits, shirts, skirts, underclothes, shoes and socks for boys and girls.

Harriet Lewis survived three years of constant challenge. In 1870, she married Edward C. Kinney, a Civil War veteran of service with Company F, 103rd Ohio Infantry. Kinney, a civil engineer, was then engaged in railroad construction in Missouri. Harriet found that the family of a civil engineer had no permanent home as she followed her husband to Canada, Mississippi, Ohio and Iowa, wherever business took him. Eventually, the Kinney family, by then with six children, moved to Denver and finally to Montana, where Edward Kinney assumed charge of a project taking water from the Gallatin River to irrigate bench land farms.

The Kinneys made their home in Bozeman, where Mrs. Harriet Lewis Kinney continued to live until her death on September 19, 1931. This Civil War Freedmen's Bureau teacher rests today in Sunset Hills Cemetery in Bozeman.

A CIVIL WAR FIGHTING TEAM:
COLONEL AND MRS. FRANCIS MALONE[20]

Women played a varied and vital role in the Civil War. Mrs. Elizabeth Casey Malone, wife of Lieutenant Colonel Francis M. Malone, followed her husband into battle, serving as a combat nurse. On her death in 1921, Elizabeth's obituary recorded that she "had the distinction of receiving from President Lincoln the only permit he ever granted, allowing a woman to accompany in the capacity of nurse, the regiment that her husband commanded." Sadly, no journal or other writings by Mrs. Malone have been found to give us details of her service as a Civil War nurse.

Francis Marion Malone was born in Toronto, Vermilion County, Indiana, on July 31, 1838, while Elizabeth Casey was born in nearby Shelby County three years later. The two were married on March 8, 1860, and settled on a farm in southern Indiana. On August 12, 1861, Francis Malone raised a company of one hundred men. Since the quota for Indiana volunteer regiments was full, Malone was assigned to the 1st Kansas Cavalry, later renamed the 7th Kansas. This unit was also known as the John Brown Jr. Regiment in honor of Captain John Brown Jr. of Ashtabula, Ohio, who commanded a company in the regiment and was the son of the martyred abolitionist. Francis Malone entered as captain of Company F, while another regimental recruit was young William F. Cody, the later renowned "Buffalo Bill."

The 1st/7th Kansas Cavalry, known also as the Independent Kansas Jayhawkers, took part in the chaotic fighting in Kansas and Missouri along the Missouri River in the region known as "Little Dixie" as the Kansas Jayhawkers fought it out with Missouri Confederate bushwhackers. During Jayhawker raids into Missouri, many slaves were freed, houses burned and plantations plundered. In 1862, the 7th was ordered to Shiloh, but before reaching that critical battle, its destination was changed to help open the railroad to Corinth, Mississippi. However, Captain Malone left the 7th on detached duty to join 32nd Illinois Infantry in the tough fighting at Shiloh. The 32nd Illinois went into action on April 6 and withstood three severe assaults. The regiment then shifted to the extreme left of Hurlbut's Division, where in heavy fighting Confederate commander General Albert Sidney Johnson was mortally wounded, leading to the Confederate defeat. The loss of the talented and charismatic Albert Sidney Johnston proved a crushing

---

20. Earlier version published in *Tribune*, April 28, 2013.

Colonel Francis Malone commanded the 1st/7th Kansas Cavalry, also known as the Kansas Independent Jayhawkers. *Author's collection.*

blow to the Confederacy in the Western Theater. After the battle, Captain Malone returned to the fighting Kansas 7th as it was assigned to a brigade commanded by Brigadier General Philip Sheridan.

In August 1863, Malone was promoted to major. During an engagement at Wyatt, Mississippi, Union forces were fighting desperately against odds, facing withering fire from a Confederate blockhouse fort. Major Malone advised his commander that he could take the stronghold by attacking with five hundred men. Permission was granted, and Major Malone led a brave charge late at night and succeeded in capturing the blockhouse. While riding near this fort, his horse fell backward into a forty-foot-deep well, pulling Major Malone in with it. Only after the battle ended the following day was he discovered and rescued, badly injured.

After another promotion and now in command of the 7th Kansas, in November 1864, Lieutenant Colonel Malone wrote to Kansas senator James Lane imploring him to use his influence with President Lincoln and the War Department to transfer the 7th back to Kansas so that Malone could recruit more Kansas men to fill the depleted ranks of his regiment. Colonel Malone wrote, "I have just returned from the Expedition after the Rebbel [*sic*] Gen [Sterling] Price, after being in the sadel Sixty two days…leading the gallant Kansas men…I commanded the regiment & have commanded in more fights…than any other man in the regiment."

After mustering out of service, Colonel Malone engaged in mining in Missouri until 1878, when he went to Colorado. Shortly after, he joined the Chicago, Milwaukee & St. Paul Railroad as traveling freight agent, and in 1883, he came to Montana as general agent for the Rocky Mountains and Pacific Coast region. The Malones lived in Helena until 1907, when he left the railroad and moved to Miles City to operate a sheep ranch in Custer County.

Just eight weeks before celebrating their sixty-first wedding anniversary, Civil War nurse Mrs. Elizabeth Malone died in Miles City in her eightieth year. Civil War veteran Colonel Francis Malone passed on in 1927, and both rest today at Elizabeth's birthplace, Pana, Illinois.

A UNION NURSE ON THE FRONT LINES IN THE CIVIL WAR: SARAH MARANDA STRONG VORUS[21]

Sarah Maranda Strong Vorus, an angel on the battlefields of the Civil War, was a most remarkable woman. A wife, mother and nurse, she came up the Missouri River by steamboat to the Sun River Valley and lived to age 102, becoming the oldest Civil War "veteran" to pass away in Montana.

Born in New York in 1840, young Sarah moved west to Boone County, Illinois, with parents James and Orpha Strong. The family settled at Belvedere, Illinois, where Sarah married John T. Vorus in 1864. Their only child, Jessie, was born on January 19, 1865, and ten days later, John Vorus was drafted and assigned to Company G, 9th Illinois Cavalry. Three of his brothers also served in this regiment.

When her husband went to war, Sarah Vorus, too, went to war. She sought direct involvement by serving as a nurse at a time when only about six thousand women served as volunteer nurses in the Union Nursing Corps organized by Dorothea Dix. Sarah Vorus experienced firsthand the grim effects of war—amputated limbs, gaping wounds, mutilated bodies. Surrounded by disease and death, Sarah and the other female and male nurses rendered critical aid to the sick and wounded on both sides. Sadly, all too few nurses recorded their experiences. These brave women of the nursing corps remain today all too historically anonymous and constitute one of the rare aspects of Civil War history.

---

21. Earlier version published in *Tribune*, March 25, 2012.

An 1864 photograph of battlefield nurses in action. *Library of Congress.*

Sarah Vorus left few words for posterity of her wartime service. No "service record" was kept for the nurses, and after the war they were not honored as veterans. We do know that on one occasion in Tennessee, Sarah and three other nurses were cut off far behind enemy lines. A Union officer gave her a horse to ride to safety to keep her from being captured by Confederate forces. Sarah kept the animal and later raised seven colts from it. Sarah long remembered, "The war was awful."

Husband John Vorus, by then promoted to corporal, was mustered out of service on October 31, 1865, in Selma, Alabama, badly crippled and disabled. John Vorus died in a veterans' hospital in Milwaukee, Wisconsin. He received an invalid pension, and Sarah later received a widow's pension for her husband's service.

In May 1876, Sarah Vorus and her eleven-year-old daughter, Jessie, departed Sioux City, Iowa, on the steamboat *General Meade* en route Fort Benton to join Sarah's parents on their ranch in the Sun River Valley. The six-week steamboat trip proved an exciting adventure, and she remembered events like "burying the deadman," a technique used to get the boat over rapids, whereby a large log was buried on the bank of the river and fastened by a rope to a small engine. The engine would wind up the rope, thus moving the boat over the rapids.

Sarah and daughter Jessie reached Fort Benton on June 27 and moved on by stagecoach to the Sun River Valley, where they joined their family, living for some years with Sarah's parents. She remembered in those days there were many saloons and an old store called the George Steell store at the town of Sun River. Nearby Fort Shaw served as headquarters for an infantry regiment, where black American soldiers (25th U.S. Infantry) were stationed before the fort closed to become an Indian Industrial School. For more than half a century, Sarah remained in the valley to see Jessie marry Byrd Alexander Robertson and raise a family of five children.

As she neared age 90, Sarah Vorus moved to Billings and entered the Montana Home for the Aged. In reminiscing shortly after her 102nd birthday in 1942, she recalled seeing President Abraham Lincoln and hearing him speak on several occasions. She remembered living in the same block with General Ulysses Grant in Belvidere. "I had tea at his house several times," she mused. Later on July 28, 1942, remarkable Civil War nurse Sarah Maranda Strong Vorus passed away. She is interred in Sun River Cemetery. With her passing, Montana lost its oldest known nurse and "veteran" of the Civil War.

A SPY FOR THE UNION:
REBECCA NORTON OF MISSOURI

Mrs. Rebecca Norton Terry, a woman with a remarkable career, died in Butte, Montana, on October 10, 1926. Born Rebecca L. Norton in Kentucky in April 1833, her early life was spent in "Henry Clay" country. Kentucky in that era was a dark and gloomy ground of hardship through numberless encounters with native Indians and attacks of malaria and other illnesses.

Noted historian Martha Edgerton Rolfe Plassmann documented Rebecca Norton Terry's remarkable life and Civil War experiences in 1926.[22]

Rebecca Norton's father was a soldier in the War of 1812 and the father of fourteen children, of whom Rebecca was the eighth. Like many Virginians and Kentuckians, Mr. Norton caught the western fever and

---

22. *Whitefish Pilot*, November 27, 1926.

moved to Missouri when Rebecca was young. He was an ardent patriot and Unionist, and being convinced that there would be a civil war, he told his children, "There will some day be a war between the North and the South but remember that you cannot be traitors to your government; it is the best on earth."

Even before the Civil War, Missouri was a battleground of the two factions: slave owners and abolitionists. Nowhere were there more bitter feelings than in Missouri. Secessionists believed they were patriots and regarded the North as untrue to the principles on which our government was founded. Force was used to decide the right or wrong of the question or at least to silence opposition.

Of Revolutionary ancestry, the Norton family took the Union side when the war broke out, with the men joining the Northern army and the women doing their part in the strife, both at home and with the troops. Missouri was in a constant state of turmoil, where contending forces surged back and forth.

Miss Norton did her part, aiding the passing Union soldiers and even acting on occasion as a spy. Union officials soon recognized her services and commended her patriotism, while she earned the hatred of her neighbors who favored the Southern cause. Of her activity as a spy, she said, "It was bad to lie, but those were times little understood now, and to be a spy was one way we had to serve our country." Shortly before the siege of Vicksburg, she engaged as an army nurse, but an attack of smallpox compelled her to resign. Yet her work for the Union did not cease. She fed and cared for Union soldiers, who but for her assistance would have perished.

Shortly after the war, Rebecca Norton married Dr. William R. Terry and went west to the booming mining town of Butte, Montana, and then on to the Jocko (now Flathead) Reservation, where Dr. Terry served as physician for both the Indians and the surrounding white settlers. From the Jocko Reservation, the Terrys moved to Anaconda, where they lived for a time before moving on to Nevada in the 1880s. There Dr. Terry died, and his widow returned to Anaconda.

Mrs. Rebecca Terry lived alone in a small house doing all her own work almost to the day of her death at the age of ninety-three. She died at the home of her niece, Mrs. Worth, of Butte, after a short illness. Rebecca Norton Terry served the Union cause in many ways.

Chapter 6

From the Civil War to the Indian Wars

T he Montana Indian Wars of the 1860s and '70s were fought by leaders trained through years of combat in the Civil War. Incidents and attacks by Lakota Sioux, Cheyenne and Arapaho along the Bozeman Trail during 1864 culminated in August 1865 with the Powder River Expedition as a punitive campaign. Though it achieved some success, it failed to defeat or intimidate the Indians, and resistance to travel on the Bozeman Trail became even more determined.

In the aftermath of the Civil War, the U.S. Army, though greatly reduced in numbers, began to move into Montana Territory to establish military posts. By 1866, the regular army was cut to fewer than thirty-five thousand men. This number grew to fifty-one thousand in 1868 but declined until its low of twenty-five thousand was reached in 1877. Despite its austere numbers, a highly experienced army fought the Indian Wars.

As the army began to build forts in Montana Territory, its leadership ranks were manned by legendary names from the Civil War—Custer, Crook, Terry, Gibbon, De Trobriand, Howard. Equally important, the ranks of senior noncommissioned officers and enlisted were filled with combat-experienced men. Some ninety soldiers received the Medal of Honor for service in Montana's Indian Wars.

The 13th U.S. Infantry Regiment established the first permanent post at Camp Cooke in May 1866 in a badly selected location on the south bank of the Missouri River at the mouth of the Judith River. In August, two companies of the 27th U.S. Infantry established Fort C.F.

1876

Fort Shaw

A 1st Sergeant of the 7th Regiment,
United States Infantry,
in Campaign dress.

Watercolor by Derek Fitz James of first sergeant of 7th Infantry Regiment at Fort Shaw, Montana Territory. *Michael Koury Collection.*

Smith on the Big Horn River, the first of three posts built to protect the Bozeman Trail.

The impractical location of Camp Cooke led to its shift in the spring of 1867 to Camp Reynolds in the Sun River Valley. Within two months, this post was renamed Fort Shaw to honor Colonel Robert Gould Shaw. Other posts would soon follow.

For the next decade, Montana Territory's military presence ranged from 700 to 2,000 men. As the Indian Wars in the territories climaxed in 1876 with the Sioux Indian War and 1877 with the Nez Perce War, troop levels increased to 3,300—still a small number spread through a large territory.

Colonel Regis de Trobriand, a French aristocrat, served well during the Civil War and came to Montana to assume command of the 13th Infantry Regiment at Fort Shaw. Young Lieutenant James H. Bradley, a youthful Civil War veteran, arrived in 1872 to become Montana's first great soldier-historian before his untimely death at the Battle of the Big Hole. Colonel John Gibbon, distinguished leader of the Iron Brigade during the Civil War, assumed command of the 7th Infantry at Fort Shaw. Colonel George Armstrong Custer, the "Boy General" from the Civil War, sought glory on the plains of southern Montana and found death. The Christian general and leader of Reconstruction's Freedmen's Bureau, General Oliver O. Howard led the army against the Nez Perce. Private Robert Loss, a German immigrant, served in the Civil War and brought his family to Montana Territory for service in the frontier army.

THE FRENCH ARISTOCRAT IN AMERICA'S CIVIL AND INDIAN WARS: COLONEL REGIS DE TROBRIAND[23]

While many Civil War veterans came to Montana Territory during and after the war for adventure and opportunity, others arrived to garrison new army posts established to protect white settlers in the early stages of Montana's Indian Wars. The post–Civil War army offered many veterans an opportunity to continue active military service. Colonel Regis de Trobriand, a man with a unique past and a hero of Civil War service, arrived at Fort Shaw, Montana Territory, on June 4, 1869, to assume command of Montana Military District and the 13th Infantry Regiment.

---

23. Earlier version published in *Tribune*, March 31, 2013.

Philippe Regis Denis de Keredern de Trobriand was born near Tours, France, on June 4, 1816, the son of a baron and general who had served in Napoleon Bonaparte's army and survived the disastrous retreat from Moscow. By age twenty-five, Regis de Trobriand had cut a wide swath through the French aristocracy as a lawyer, poet, novelist and expert swordsman, survivor of several duels. In 1841, he immigrated to the United States, joined the social elite in New York City and began a career writing and editing French-language publications.

Early in the Civil War, Trobriand assumed command of the 55th New York Infantry, a predominantly French-immigrant regiment known as the Lafayette Guards. In late 1862, the 55th and 38th New York regiments were merged, and Trobriand became colonel of the new 38th. After the Battle of Chancellorsville in May 1863, he was named to command a new brigade. The highlight of Trobriand's war came at Gettysburg. On the second day of the battle, his brigade took up positions in the Wheatfield. Throughout the day, his brigade stood strong against powerful assaults by General John Bell Hood's division, composed of two brigades. Trobriand's men held throughout the day but at a terrible price, with every third man a casualty.

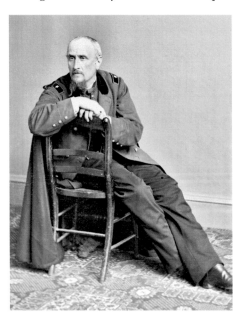

Based on his impressive leadership at Gettysburg, Trobriand was promoted to brigadier general. He led a division during the Petersburg and Appomattox campaigns. As the war was ending, on April 9, 1865, Trobriand was appointed to brevet major general.

After the Civil War, Trobriand remained in the army and, in June 1867, was assigned to command Fort Stevenson, Dakota Territory, with a peacetime rank of colonel. Receiving news of his appointment while in France on vacation, he wrote in his diary:

Brigadier General Philippe Regis de Trobriand, Civil War hero, commanded Fort Shaw, Montana Territory, in 1869–70 during the Marias massacre. *Library of Congress.*

I left Paris to go straight to the Upper Missouri. From the brilliant peaks of civilized life, I was to plunge straight into the dark pit of savage existence. Never was there a greater contrast, but contrasts are the spice of life; they banish monotony and boredom, and give life a variety that cannot be found in a settled existence.

Regis de Trobriand came west as a writer and artist as well as a soldier. While serving at Fort Stevenson, Colonel Trobriand kept a diary that formed the basis for an important book on the upper Missouri frontier, *Military Life in Dakota*. His experiences in Dakota Territory facing constant Sioux Indian incidents prepared Colonel Trobriand for his next assignment as commander of Montana Military District.

Colonel Trobriand reported to Fort Shaw on June 4, 1869, at the culmination of incidents between white settlers and Blackfoot Indians extending through the previous five years, principally at Fort Benton and along the Benton Road to Helena. Just ten weeks after Colonel Trobriand's arrival, legendary fur trader Malcolm Clarke was murdered at his ranch on Little Prickly Pear Creek by five Piegan Blackfeet led by Owl Child, a relative of Clarke's wife. In his official report, Colonel Trobriand presented a thoughtful summary of the situation, noting that most Blackfoot Indians remained "still perfectly quiet" and that the recent hostilities rested primarily on a renegade band of Piegans.

Most noteworthy of Colonel Trobriand's service in Montana was the January 1870 Marias campaign. Colonel Trobriand was ordered to strike the Piegan Blackfeet hard in winter camp on the Marias River. In the tragic fog of war, Major Eugene Baker attacked the wrong camp, not that of trouble-making Mountain Chief but rather that of the peacefully inclined Heavy Runner. This crushing blow effectively brought an end to Piegan incidents against white settlers.

Later in 1870, Colonel de Trobriand was reassigned to duty in the South, to New Orleans in the latter days of Reconstruction. This French aristocrat of many talents, including Civil War and Indian War leadership, lived his last years at Bayport, New York, passing on July 15, 1897.

MONTANA'S FIRST GREAT HISTORIAN: GALLANT LIEUTENANT JAMES H. BRADLEY

Lieutenant James H. Bradley, a man of many talents and a Civil War soldier, was Montana's finest early historian before his tragic death in 1877 at the Battle of the Big Hole during the Nez Perce War.

Lieutenant James Bradley, Montana's first great historian, was killed at the Battle of the Big Hole. *Overholser Historical Research Center.*

Born in Ohio in 1844, at the outbreak of the Civil War in April 1861, Bradley joined the 14th Ohio Infantry at age sixteen. During his three months' service with the 14th, Private Bradley took part in actions at Philippi, Laurel Hill and Carrick's Ford, (West) Virginia. Mustered out in August 1861, he entered Oberlin College but decided he could not sit out the war, so he enlisted in Company F, 45th Ohio Infantry, in June 1862 to serve through the rest of the war. Bradley was promoted to full corporal on January 14, 1863, and was captured in a skirmish near Philadelphia, Tennessee, in October. Imprisoned at Andersonville, Georgia, for six months, he survived that ordeal to be released through a prisoner exchange. Corporal Bradley rejoined his regiment and fought in the battles of Kennesaw Mountain, Peachtree Creek, Jonesborough and the siege of Atlanta. He was promoted full sergeant in February 1865 and mustered out June 12.

Commissioned second lieutenant in the 18th U.S. Infantry in April 1866, Lieutenant Bradley's first duty post was Fort Phil Kearny in Powder River country protecting the Bozeman Trail during the Red Cloud War. After rapid promotion to first lieutenant in August 1867, Bradley was transferred to Reconstruction duty in Atlanta where he met his future wife, Mary Beach.

Joining Company B, 7th Infantry Regiment, at Fort Shaw in March 1871, Lieutenant Bradley and his company were assigned to Fort Benton Military Post the following year. There, Lieutenant Bradley handled his military duties with ease and often served as post commander. He had an insatiable curiosity and focused his interests on science and history. As he talked to the old-timers in Fort Benton, he wrote their stories as a labor of love and with the skill of an experienced historian. In the span of three years, Lieutenant Bradley assembled a remarkable record of diaries, journals and letters from his research, forming more than eleven volumes of historical writings. The right man in the right place, Bradley's monumental contribution to Montana history recorded unique information on the early history of Fort Benton and the territory, the fur trade of the Missouri and Yellowstone Valleys and the Indian tribes of the region.

Bradley's years in Fort Benton spanned a critical stage in the evolution of the head of navigation on the Missouri River as it emerged from the fur- and robe-trading era toward an emerging frontier merchant town. At this time, white women and children began arriving in Fort Benton, among them Bradley's wife, Mrs. Mary Beach Bradley. The great fur traders of the upper Missouri—Alexander Culbertson, Joseph Kipp and others—still lived around Fort Benton. Pioneer merchants like T.C. Power, I.G. Baker, William G. and Charlie Conrad and others found Lieutenant Bradley an inquiring and thorough chronicler of their experiences and anecdotes. The many encounters between Native Americans and newly arriving miners and settlers of the past decade were still fresh in the memories of the town's inhabitants.

Company B remained in Fort Benton until September 1, 1875, when it returned to Fort Shaw. With Montana's most violent Indian Wars breaking out, tension and separation filled life at Fort Shaw. On March 17, 1876, a battalion of the 7th Infantry, known as the Montana Column, under Colonel John Gibbon, with Lieutenant Bradley commanding a mounted detachment, left Fort Shaw to join the Yellowstone Expedition against the Sioux Indians. In one of the ironies of this campaign, at the very time Custer's men were being overwhelmed, the Montana Column could find very little action. Lieutenant Bradley's mounted troops were the first to discover the dead of Custer's command on the Little Big Horn in late June. Bradley chronicled this campaign in a journal that proved his skill as an observer and writer. His journal was first published in 1896 in volume 2, *Contributions to the Historical Society of Montana*, and later in book form, *The March of the Montana Column: A Prelude to the Custer Disaster*. The Montana Column returned to Fort Shaw on October 6, 1876, and remained in garrison over the winter.

In late July 1877, Colonel Gibbon and the 7th Infantry departed Fort Shaw to intercept the Nez Perce in western Montana. On August 9 at the Battle of the Big Hole, Lieutenant Bradley was killed in action leading an assault by his mounted detachment on the Nez Perce camp. The life of gallant Lieutenant James H. Bradley—young Civil War soldier, survivor of Andersonville, Indian Wars leader and Montana's greatest early historian—tragically was cut short. Yet scholars today still recognize Bradley's historical material as literary gold.

FROM THE IRON BRIGADE TO THE MONTANA INDIAN WARS: COLONEL JOHN GIBBON

Colonel John Gibbon, from the Iron Brigade to the Montana Indian Wars. *Library of Congress.*

John Gibbon emerged from the Civil War with a reputation for success. After all, his men of the Iron Brigade fought tenaciously at Antietam, bore the brunt of Pickett-Pettigrew-Trimble's Charge and could not be broken at Gettysburg. His service continued in the Indian Wars with the frontier army in Montana Territory, where his 7th Infantry Regiment participated in the Sioux Indian War of 1876 and the Nez Perce War of 1877.

John Oliver Gibbon was born on April 20, 1827, in today's Philadelphia, although his family early on moved to North Carolina. He graduated from the Military Academy, an average student. After service with the 3rd U.S. Artillery, Lieutenant Gibbon was assigned as instructor at the Military Academy, where he authored *The Artillerist's Manual*, a textbook used by both North and South in the Civil War and by the army for decades after.

Captain Gibbon's family split loyalties at the outbreak of the Civil War. He remained loyal to the Union, while his three brothers and two brothers-in-law joined the Confederacy. Returning to Washington, D.C., in October 1861 from army duty in Utah, Captain Gibbon became chief of artillery for Brigadier General Irvin McDowell's division, training four volunteer batteries.

In May 1862, Gibbon was appointed brigadier general of U.S. Volunteers and was assigned to command a brigade. Both General Gibbon and his brigade gained great respect for their performance at battles ranging from Second Bull Run to Antietam. At the Battle of South Mountain, Major General Joseph Hooker exclaimed that Gibbon's men "fought like iron," and from that came the sobriquet "Iron Brigade." At the Battle of Antietam, Gibbon personally manned an artillery gun as both cannoneer and gunner in the bloody fighting at the Cornfield. Brigadier General Edward S. Bragg of Wisconsin observed Gibbon's leadership in battle:

> *General Gibbon stood up with his command, face to face, against the flower of ["Stonewall"] Jackson's corps—and strong and chivalrous was the fore, hand to hand almost, was the battle of that night. And then there it was that Jackson's stubborn fighters learned that iron was as enduring and immovable as stone.*

Wounded while leading a division at Fredericksburg, Gibbon returned to action commanding Second Division, Second Corps, at Chancellorsville and Gettysburg. At Gettysburg, his division bore the brunt of fighting during Pickett-Pettigrew-Trimble's Charge, and a bullet struck his left shoulder. After four months' convalescence, Gibbon returned to duty, and the following spring, he resumed command of his division, leading them in the bloody campaign against Richmond.

In June 1864, Gibbon was promoted major general of U.S. Volunteers and assumed command of Twenty-Four Corps, leading his men in the final operations against the Army of Northern Virginia. At Appomattox Court House, he was one of three commissioners selected by General Grant to arrange details of the surrender.

Remaining in the postwar army, he was promoted to colonel of the 36th U.S. Infantry Regiment. In 1870, Colonel Gibbon assumed command of the 7th Infantry at Fort Shaw. During this decisive stage of the Montana Indian Wars, Colonel Gibbon commanded the Montana Column that discovered and rescued the survivors and buried the dead of Lieutenant Colonel George A. Custer's 7th Cavalry after the Battle of the Little Bighorn. Gibbon attacked the Nez Perce at Big Hole, and while tactically defeated, his outnumbered force inflicted substantial losses on the Nez Perce. In later action, elements of the 7th Infantry with civilian volunteers fought delaying action against the Nez Perce as they crossed the Missouri River at Cow Island and Cow Creek Canyon.

Military historian Michael Koury believes that Colonel Gibbon was a more experienced Indian campaigner than was General Alfred Terry. Koury states that Gibbon's account of the Sioux campaign of 1876 presents "a much clearer picture of the extreme difficulty of executing a campaign against hostile Indians in virtually unmapped terrain."

Colonel John Gibbon passed on February 6, 1896, and is buried at Arlington National Cemetery. Survivors of his Iron Brigade took up a collection for a modest monument for their highly respected Civil War commander.

Dreams of Grandeur on the Backs of His Men: George Armstrong Custer

Flamboyant George Armstrong Custer lived and died by the sword. By June 1863 during the Civil War, he had risen from lieutenant to the "Boy General" of cavalry volunteers at age twenty-three. Weeks later, Brigadier General Custer's two thousand cavalrymen, although outnumbered three to one, fought the Confederate cavalry to a standstill at East Cavalry Field in one of the decisive actions on the critical third day at Gettysburg. Thirteen years later, he and his men lay dead on the rolling hills of the Little Big Horn.

George A. Custer was born in Ohio on December 5, 1839. Raised in Ohio and Michigan, he entered the U.S. Military Academy in 1858 and graduated last in his class of thirty-four in June 1861. From the First Battle of Bull Run through the end of the war, he built a strong reputation as the most dashing, daring and effective Union cavalry general.

As he later wrote, his dreams of grandeur were being fulfilled:

> *In years long-numbered with the past, when I was verging upon manhood, my every thought was ambitious—not to be wealthy, not to be learned,*

Monochrome halftone print by William Montague Cary of the last ride of Colonel George Armstrong Custer and his 7th Cavalry. *Author's collection.*

but to be great. I desired to link my name with acts & men, and in such a manner as to be a mark of honor—not only to the present, but to future generations. George Armstrong Custer.

In the assessment of historian Stephen Ambrose, "Custer rode to the top of his profession over the backs of his fallen soldiers." Custer's first instinct always was to charge the enemy on every field of battle, no matter what odds he faced. Ambrose wrote:

Throughout his military career he indulged that instinct whenever he faced opposition. Neither a thinker nor a planner, Custer scorned maneuvering, reconnaissance, and all other subtleties of warfare. He was a good, if often reckless, small-unit combat commander, no more and no less. But his charges, although by no means always successful, made him a favorite of the national press and one of the superstars of his day. He and [wife] Libbie came to rank high on the Washington social list of sought-after couples.

Personally fearless, Custer accepted every risk and passed it along to his men as they fought their way through most of the major battles of the Army of the Potomac in the Eastern Theater. Custer became a major general in September 1864 and took command of the Third Cavalry Division, operating effectively under Major General Philip Sheridan. In April 1865, Union cavalry pursued General Robert E. Lee as he began his retreat to Appomattox Court House. Custer's Third Division blocked Lee's retreat on its final day and received the first flag of truce from the Confederates. Custer was present at Lee's surrender, and General Sheridan presented the surrender-signing table as a gift for Custer's wife with a note to her praising her husband's gallantry.

After war's end, Custer was appointed lieutenant colonel in the newly created 7th U.S. Cavalry Regiment. For the next decade, he took part in expeditions against the Cheyenne and Lakota Sioux, including the Battle of Washita River in 1868 and the Black Hills Expedition in 1874. Custer's announcement of the discovery of gold in the Black Hills triggered that gold rush.

Violence escalated with the Cheyenne and Lakota Sioux as treaties were broken through the Black Hills gold rush. Remaining "free" Indians were ordered to designated reservations. In response, the Lakota, Northern Cheyenne and Arapaho Indians formed a united encampment. Custer's 7th Cavalry departed Fort Abraham Lincoln on May 17, 1876, as part of a larger army force under General Alfred Terry that included Colonel Gibbon's Montana Column.

The Battle of the Little Big Horn on June 25 led to the death of George Armstrong Custer and some 210 of his men. True to his instincts during the Civil War, Colonel Custer charged his men into battle regardless of odds. Custer's name is linked indelibly to the Battle of the Little Big Horn "not only to the present, but to future generations."

The Christian General and Leader of Lincoln's "Unfinished Work": O.O. Howard

If the Civil War was about unity and freedom, Oliver Otis Howard was a true hero during and after the war. He had his detractors and to some earned the nickname "Uh Oh Howard," but his record reveals a Godly man who performed bravely during the war and then accepted the impossible challenge of leading the social revolution for the newly freed slaves. Above all, Otis Howard was a man of principle who believed the end of the war simply began the "unfinished work" mentioned in President Lincoln's Gettysburg Address.

Born on November 8, 1830, in Leeds, Maine, Oliver O. Howard graduated from Bowdoin College in 1850 and the Military Academy in 1854, fourth in his class of thirty-eight. As a second lieutenant, he married Elizabeth Anne Waite in 1855 and two years later served in the Seminole Wars. It was in Florida that he experienced conversion to evangelical Christianity, which would guide him for the rest of his life. He became an ardent abolitionist.

As the army hastily organized early in the Civil War, Howard was appointed colonel of the 3rd Maine Infantry Regiment and temporarily commanded a brigade at the First Battle of Bull Run. Promoted to brigadier general, he led his brigade in the Battle at Fair Oaks on June 1, 1862. He received the Medal of Honor for his bravery at Fair Oaks, the largest battle to date in the Eastern Theater. His citation emphasized, "Brigadier General Howard led the 61st New York Infantry in a charge in which he was twice severely wounded in the right arm, necessitating amputation."

Within months, he was back in action in time to participate in Antietam. Promoted to major general and assigned to command Eleventh Corps, composed largely of German immigrants. Howard suffered his first major reverse when Lieutenant General Stonewall Jackson's men routed his new Eleventh Corps at Chancellorsville. Back in action two months later at Gettysburg, his battered corps again was driven back, but recovering, Howard wisely selected Cemetery Hill as the key defensive position, and his men withstood heavy assaults for the next two days.

Howard and Eleventh Corps were transferred to the Western Theater for the rest of the war. In July 1864, Howard assumed command of the Army of Tennessee, fighting in the Atlanta Campaign and Sherman's March to the Sea.

A "practical abolitionist" who believed the freed slaves deserved equality and needed education and employment, from May 1865 to July 1874, Howard led the Freedmen's Bureau. Charged with integrating freed slaves into society during the Reconstruction era, Howard implemented a wide range of social programs, including

Brigadier General Oliver Otis Howard, the Christian general and leader of the freedmen. *Library of Congress.*

education, medical care and food distribution. Backed by Radical Republicans in Congress, Howard clashed repeatedly with President Andrew Johnson. Knowing that the freed slaves needed jobs, Howard ordered his bureau to lease confiscated and abandoned Confederate lands in forty-acre plots to ex-slaves. Unfortunately, President Johnson rescinded Howard's order.

Criticism of Howard came from every direction, from ex-Confederates for his strong action to help freedmen and from abolitionists and freedmen for his lack of success. All the while, sentiment in the country was shifting against Reconstruction and toward accommodation with former Confederates. Despite his untenable situation, Howard bravely did everything in his power to educate and help the freedmen. Former slave Sojourner Truth wrote to Howard saying she heard "people saying for you and against you. I speak in behalf of you, knowing what you have done in behalf of my poor race." In fact, Howard's Freedmen's Bureau fed millions, built many hospitals, negotiated labor contracts and established many schools and training institutes for blacks, including

Howard University, named for the general. He did his best against impossible odds.

In 1874, Brigadier General Howard assumed command of the Department of the Columbia in Washington Territory. He took part in the Indian Wars, and in 1877, he mounted the campaign in Montana against the Nez Perce that resulted in the capture of Chief Joseph and many of the Nez Perce at the Battle of the Bear's Paw, ending the Nez Perce saga along their trail of courage.

Historian Robert Utley assessed that Howard's leadership against the Apaches in 1872, the Nez Perce in 1877, the Bannocks and Paiutes in 1878 and the Sheepeaters in 1879 all added up to an impressive record. True to his nature, at the Bear's Paw when Chief Joseph tried to hand his rifle to him, General Howard motioned that this symbol of surrender instead should go to Colonel Nelson Miles.

Returning east in 1881, Howard served as superintendent at West Point and other command assignments before retiring in 1894. Oliver Otis Howard, Christian general and champion of freedmen, died on October 26, 1909, and rests today at Lake View Cemetery in Burlington, Vermont.

FROM PRUSSIA TO FRONTIER MONTANA VIA THE CIVIL AND INDIAN WARS: MUSICIAN ROBERT F. LOSS[24]

It's a long way from Prussia (in today's Germany) to Missouri, yet Robert F. Loss and many other Germans crossed the Atlantic Ocean to settle in St. Louis. Born Robert Lass in 1847, he came to America with his family at age six. Robert Loss served in both the Civil War and the Indian Wars before settling down to ranching near St. Peter's Mission in Cascade County, Montana Territory.

Like many German immigrants, Loss joined the Union army to fight in the Civil War. Because of his youth (six weeks short of sixteen years of age), Loss enlisted in St. Louis on February 23, 1863, as a bugler, and he was assigned to Company A, 11th Missouri Cavalry.

After serving briefly in New Mexico and Arizona, Company A returned to Missouri and took part in skirmishes in Arkansas at Spring Town, Waugh's Farm near Batesville, Little Red River and Jacksonport. Typical

---

24. Earlier version published in *Tribune*, June 24, 2012.

of the chaotic conditions in Missouri and Arkansas at this time, when the 11th Missouri Cavalry and supporting units entered the Batesville area, they faced Confederate guerrilla units and outlaw elements preying on small Union detachments. At Lewis Waugh's farm, a wagon train escorted by the 11th Missouri Cavalry and 4th Arkansas Mounted was ambushed, resulting in forty-six casualties. During 1865, the 11th Missouri Cavalry was ordered to Little Rock, and Private Loss was discharged on February 22. By war's end, the 11th Missouri Cavalry had traveled over ten thousand miles during its various expeditions.

By September 1865, Private Loss was back in the army, enlisting in Company H, 18th U.S. Infantry. For three years, Loss served in the 18th Infantry in the Mountain District, Department of the Platte, under Colonel Henry B. Carrington stationed at Fort Phil Kearny, Nebraska. During the last year of his service, the 18th Infantry was assigned to protect the Union Pacific Railroad as the first transcontinental railroad neared completion.

On right with his family, Private Robert F. Loss, 11th Missouri Cavalry (Union), continued in the army after the Civil War and served at Fort Shaw, Montana Territory. *Clint Loss Collection.*

In July 1869, Robert Loss joined the 3rd U.S. Infantry Regiment. Initially assigned to Company H, Loss transferred to the band, where he played violin for many years. While the regiment was stationed at Fort Wallace, Kansas, Loss married Annie Crosby. In the summer of 1878, the 3rd Infantry relieved the 7th Infantry at Fort Shaw. Private Loss arrived there with his wife, three children and daughter Minnie from his wife's previous marriage. For six years, musician Loss performed in many band and orchestral concerts as an integral part of the social life of Fort Shaw and local communities. A glimpse of the Fort Shaw musical scene at this time comes from an officer's wife, Mrs. Frances Roe, when she wrote, "Our little entertainment...was a wonderful success. Every seat was occupied, every corner packed, and we were afraid that the old theater might collapse...the fine orchestra of twenty pieces was a great addition and support."

When Robert Loss retired from the army on July 15, 1884, his discharge noted his "excellent character." The Loss family homesteaded on Saint John's Creek near St. Peter's Mission, where in 1891 he received patent to 160 acres and built a six-room log house used by the family until 1932.

After ranching for many years, Robert and Annie Loss moved to the town of Cascade. In May 1935, Governor F.H. Cooney appointed Loss to the board of the Montana State Soldiers Home. When he died in Cascade on April 2, 1936, he was one of the last remaining Civil War veterans in Cascade County. Robert Loss served well during the Civil War and Montana's Indian Wars and today rests in Cascade's Hillside Cemetery.

Chapter 7

The Legend of Victory and the Lost Cause Live On

Within a year after the end of the Civil War, the myth of the Lost Cause surfaced. Edward A. Pollard, wartime editor of the *Richmond Examiner*, coined the term "Lost Cause" in 1866 when he published *The Lost Cause: A New Southern History of the War of the Confederates*. The Lost Cause was further developed by United Confederate Veterans and other white Southerners, many of them former Confederate generals, who sought to present the war in the best possible light for the Confederacy. Dwelling on the postwar climate of economic and racial uncertainty, the Lost Cause romanticized the "Old South" and the Confederate war effort while tending to distort history by collectively ignoring the horrors of slavery. Having lost the war, the South was determined to "win" the peace on its terms. The myth of the Lost Cause provided a sense of relief to white Southerners concerned about dishonor in their defeat, and many white Americans found it a useful tool in reconciling North and South and unifying the nation.

Even before the end of the war, Southern women were transforming their wartime soldiers and associations to memorialize their Lost Cause in the public memory. Nostalgia for the "Old South" influenced entertainment such as popular minstrel shows for many decades. Other entertainment such as books like *The Clansman* and movies like *Birth of a Nation* continued the powerful myth.

Counter-Reconstruction prevailed throughout the South by the 1880s as Jim Crow laws institutionalized segregation and discrimination. Some

African Americans migrated to Montana and elsewhere in the West to seek safer and more open societies. What they found was a milder but still pervasive form of discrimination that would not break down until the 1950s–60s. The dedication in Helena, Montana's capital, in 1916 of a Confederate monument was symptomatic of the lingering myth of the Lost Cause far beyond the South. During the early 1920s, the Ku Klux Klan experienced an increased presence in the North and in Montana.

United Confederate Veterans (UCV) were active in Montana for many years. In 1902, two Montanans attended the Twelfth Annual Meeting and Reunion of UCV in Dallas, Texas: Northwest Division commander Major General Frank D. Brown and Montana Brigade commander Brigadier General Paul A. Fusz, both of Philipsburg. Today, the Sons of Confederate Veterans are active nationally with some members in Montana, although there are not camps active in the state. The United Daughters of the Confederacy (UDC) continued activities well into the twentieth century.

The Grand Army of the Republic (GAR), founded in 1866 in Decatur, Illinois, emerged as the most powerful fraternal organization for Union veterans serving in the war. Formed on the principles of "Fraternity, Charity and Loyalty," it grew as a de facto political arm of the Republican Party during Reconstruction. The GAR reached a peak membership of almost 500,000 and organized to support voting rights for black veterans, pensions for veterans and election of Republican political candidates. Five GAR members were elected president of the United States by 1900.

National Encampments were held every year from 1866 to 1949. The GAR was dissolved in 1956 upon the death of its last member, but it had long been succeeded by the Sons of Union Veterans of the Civil War, composed of male descendants of Union veterans. The Woman's Relief Corp Auxiliary and the Daughters of Union Veterans of the Civil War formed for women to support the GAR.

By the mid-1880s, Montana's GAR had organized as a department with posts at the local level throughout the state. Leaders like Medal of Honor recipient J.O. Gregg led Sheridan Post No. 18 in Great Falls and the Montana Department during the 1890s. Eventually, Montana organized thirty GAR posts in towns large and small throughout the state.

GRAND ARMY OF THE REPUBLIC
DEPARTMENT OF MONTANA

John Buford Post No. 1	Fort Custer
Lincoln Post No. 2	Butte City
Wadsworth Post No. 3	Helena
George H. Thomas Post No. 4	Deer Lodge
Custer Post No. 5	Sheridan/Columbia Falls
Francis P. Blair Post No. 6	Virginia City
Farragut Post No. 7	Livingston
Steadman Post No. 8	Dillon
Unknown Post No. 9	Willis
William English Post No. 10	Bozeman
Fred Winthrop Post No. 11	Missoula
Thomas L. Kane Post No. 12	Glendive
James B. McPherson No. 13	Boulder
U.S. Grant Post No. 14	Miles City
John A. Logan Post No. 15	Billings
George G. Meade Post No 16	Anaconda
Thomas Francis Meagher Post No. 17	White Sulphur Springs
Sheridan Post No. 18	Great Falls
James A. Shields Post No. 19	Lewistown
G.K. Warren Post No. 20	Fort Benton
John C. Fremont Post No. 21	Grantsdale/Hamilton
Burnside Post No. 22	Philipsburg
Nathaniel Lyon Post No. 23	Kalispell
George B. McClellan Post No. 24	Columbia Falls
Moody Post No. 25	Ennis
Garfield Post No. 26	Carlton
John A. Logan Post No. 27	Plains
William McKinley Post No. 28	Billings
George W. Jackson Post No. 29	Red Lodge
J.B. McPherson Post No. 30	Kalispell

Active today is Camp Chapman/Compliment #2 (Montana) of the Department of Colorado/Wyoming of Sons of Union Veterans of the Civil War.

Ironically, although there is a Confederate Monument in Helena, Montana, there are no GAR monuments in Montana. On the grounds of the Montana State Capitol stands a heroic statue of Union general Thomas Francis Meagher on horseback leading his Irish Brigade into battle.

GREAT FALLS HIGHLAND CEMETERY HONORS THE BLUE AND THE GRAY[25]

An exceptional monument stands front and center in Highland Cemetery in Great Falls, Montana. Soldiers Monument, dedicated on May 30, 1901, to honor those who died in service of our country, is nationally unique—it is the first monument in the United States dedicated to honor both the fallen soldiers of the blue (Union) and the gray (Confederacy).

Highland Cemetery, now called Old Highland, was formed in 1888 in time for Decoration Day, May 30, 1889. Memorial Day was originally called Decoration Day, a day to remember those who died in service during the Civil War. This day of honor was first observed on May 30, 1868, when flowers were placed on the graves of Union and Confederate soldiers at

Soldiers Plot at Highland Cemetery, Great Falls, Montana. *Author's collection.*

25. Earlier version published in *Tribune*, May 27, 2012.

Soldiers Monument at Highland Cemetery, Great Falls, Montana—first tribute in the nation to both the blue and the gray. *Author's collection.*

Arlington National Cemetery. By the twentieth century, Memorial Day had been extended to honor all Americans who died in all wars.

In 1895, local veterans of the GAR, together with Confederate veterans, formed a committee to prepare a soldiers' monument at the cemetery. Captain Joseph O. Gregg, Medal of Honor veteran, chaired the committee as it first selected a Veterans Plot for the monument, half an acre to the right of the original entrance to the cemetery.

A key part of the monument arrived in Great Falls in October 1897: an eight-inch Columbiad cannon to surmount the monument of sandstone. The cannon was cast at Watervliet Arsenal, New York, in 1858; sent to Norfolk, Virginia, in 1860; and appropriately captured, recaptured and fired by both the South and North during the war. At war's end, the cannon was transferred to New York Harbor, where it mounted guard until moved to make way for the Statue of Liberty.

Soldiers Monument, completed in 1901, is ten feet square at its base and from the ground to the muzzle of the cannon is fifteen feet high. It is

Honoring Union soldiers "To the Boys in Blue" and "To the Boys in Gray." *Author's Collection.*

constructed of cream-colored local sandstone with a tablet of pink Tennessee marble placed on each side. The tablet in front (east) and directly under the muzzle tells the history of the gun. Of the other three tablets, the one on the north bears the inscription, "IN MEMORY OF THE BOYS WHO WORE THE BLUE 1861–1865." The south tablet reads, "THE BOYS WHO WORE THE GRAY," and the tablet on the west is inscribed, "IN MEMORY OF THE BOYS OF 1898–1900 THE INDIAN WARS AND REGULAR SERVICE."

As a final touch, a copper box shaped to fit the bore of the gun was slipped into place with an iron plug dipped into red lead and driven into the muzzle with a sledge. Hermetically sealed in this box were many letters, including one from Confederate general James Longstreet, as well as photographs and newspapers.

A dedication was held Memorial Day, May 30, 1901. Governor Joseph K. Toole attended the ceremony with an elaborate program honoring forty deceased veterans whose bodies had been laid to rest in circular rows around the monument—Union veterans interred on the north and Confederates on the south.

Unveiling Soldiers Monument were six children related to and representing Union veterans; Confederate veterans; Spanish and Philippine war veterans; U.S. Army soldiers; and Indian participants in Indian Wars in Montana and regular army service in Montana.

Captain J.O. Gregg, past Montana Department commander of the GAR and chairman of the committee, dedicated the monument for the veterans with these words:

> *I dedicate it to the memory of those who in the navy guarded our inland seas and ocean coasts, and fell in defense of the flag.*

I dedicate it to the memory of those who in the army fought for our hillsides, valleys and plains, and fell in the defense of the flag.

I dedicate it to the memory of those who on land and sea fought for our union, and fell in defense of the flag; for those on land and sea who fought for the authority of the constitution.

I dedicate it to the memory of our fellow-citizens, the confederate veterans, who on land and sea fought for the South, and fell in its defense.

Comrades, salute the dead!

As you visit Highland Cemetery in Great Falls, look toward Soldiers Monument with its tablets honoring Civil War veterans, Union and Confederate. You are viewing history during this 150th anniversary of the Civil War.

RIVERSIDE CEMETERY HONORS CIVIL WAR VETERANS: THE BLUE AND THE GRAY[26]

Beautiful Riverside Cemetery on the northern bluffs above Fort Benton was formed in 1883, in time for Decoration Day on May 30. That Decoration Day, the *River Press* reported in moving terms:

Decoration Day is here again, diverting our thoughts once more from the present and calling us to an affectionate remembrance of the brave men who laid down their lives so willingly in the great civil war. It is not the privilege of many of us here to lay wreaths upon the graves of friends or relatives who fell in the mighty conflict. The roar of the blood-red tide of war was hardly heard in this distant country. The bones of our dead soldiers repose thousands of miles away, under the thickets of the wilderness, upon the slopes of Gettysburg, about Vicksburg, and at Shiloh...It is not our privilege...to scatter flowers over their honored graves. We can, however, upon this day, when time has subdued and chastened grief, when animosities are silenced, look back calmly upon the war. If many perished, what splendid valor was displayed; if many suffered, what nobility of character was developed; if blood and treasure were squandered, what glory was won; if hearts were broken, what a glorious principle was established.

---

26. Earlier version published in *River Press*, May 30, 2012.

The evil effects have passed away. Peace, and good fellowship and brotherly love have returned; and may their benign influence never be dispelled by the words of scheming demagogues. To the boys in blue, and the boys in gray, who so nobly gave their lives for the maintenance of principle and country, our minds should go back with equal love and admiration.

> *Under the rain and dew,*
> *Waiting the Judgment day,*
> *Under the roses the Blue,*
> *Under the lilies the Gray.*

Two decades after the end of the war, both North and South began to join in observing Memorial Day, and in 1886, the *River Press* reported:

The beautiful custom of decorating the graves of the soldiers who died during the great civil war has now become a national affair and is observed by both north and south alike. Its observance has done as much to heal the breach between the opposing sections as any other one thing. "One touch of nature makes the whole world kin," and the graves of northern soldiers who are buried on southern soil are receiving the same kind attention that is bestowed on the Confederate dead. The southern soldier who fought for a principle and whose body is interred in the north is not passed by, and the flowers surmount his tomb. Sectional feeling is giving way to the idea of one country.

Riverside Cemetery Veterans Plot, Fort Benton, Montana. *Author's collection.*

On Decoration Day 1890, Fort Benton went all out with an impressive procession and line of march through town. Marshal of the Day Tom J. Todd led the formation, followed by the 20th U.S. Infantry Band from Fort Assinniboine under Chief Musician J. Kunzel and members of G.K. Warren Post No. 20, GAR, under Post Commander John C. Duff, lieutenant, Company F, 30th Massachusetts Infantry. Members included, from the first platoon, George W. Crane, commanding, and Comrades Patrick Whalen, Company F, 151st Indiana Infantry; Hugh W. Patton, Company F, 53rd Pennsylvania; Robert S. Culbertson; Richard Smith, Company A, 191st New York Infantry; Dan Dutro; and Lott C. Hilton, Company F, 6th Michigan Infantry. From the second platoon, W. Gould Smith commanding and Comrades Claude B. Hamilton, sergeant Company B, 14th U.S. Cavalry; Isaac Clark, 14th Michigan Infantry; Claus Peters, musician, 6th U.S. Infantry; Oscar Parsons, Company F, 152nd Indiana Infantry; William H. Lytton, Company B, 3rd Iowa Infantry; and Terhofstedde. From the third platoon, Thomas A. Cummings, commanding, and Comrades Isaac G. McCord, Company H, 3rd California Infantry; Thomas Coatsworth; John S. Murphy, Company G, 14th New York Infantry; Wheeler O. Dexter, Company F, 16th New York Heavy Artillery; Fulkoot; and Kennedy. Others in the march included the Choteau Hose Company under Foreman J.P. Lee, Juvenile Hose Company under Assistant Foreman H.P. Stanford, pupils of the public school in charge of Professor Danks and citizens on foot and in carriages. The procession proceeded to the school buildings. From there, carriages took the band, the GAR and others to Riverside Cemetery. The GAR decorated the graves of Civil War veterans. The archway leading into the cemetery was festooned with evergreens and the graves of the dead veterans covered with the same emblems of eternal life.

By 1892, the *River Press* had begun using the name Memorial Day in place of Decoration Day. That Memorial Day, a large crowd assembled for memorial exercises at the cemetery and assisted in paying tribute to the memory of the nation's departed dead. G.K. Warren Post of the GAR and the Woman's Relief Corps performed memorial rites, and flowers were strewn on veterans' graves. In the evening, a crowd filled the courthouse to overflowing to hear a program of addresses, vocal music and recitations.

By the end of the nineteenth century, veterans had died also in the Indian Wars and in the Spanish-American War and Philippines insurrection, and Memorial Day broadened to honor veterans of all wars.

Today, Riverside Cemetery is home to veterans from many wars. Veterans of later wars are buried in Military Plot, where there are gravestones from the Spanish-American War, World War I, World War II, Vietnam and Persian Gulf. No Civil War veterans are buried in the Military Plot, but a walk around the cemetery will find the white marble curved top stones of at least sixteen Civil War Union veterans. Confederate veterans like Paul Schoonover, Company I, 28th Virginia Infantry, have angled top stones. The well cared for grounds of Riverside Cemetery provide a fine home for the blue and the gray from Chouteau County.

CHOUTEAU COUNTY CIVIL WAR VETERANS AND THE GRAND ARMY OF THE REPUBLIC[27]

The Civil War came at a time when the West was undergoing settlement by nonnative's, although Fort Benton had long been a trading outpost on the upper Missouri. Many veterans, both Union and Confederate, came to the head of navigation on the Missouri to start new lives during and after the Civil War.

By 1885, Fort Benton was home for many Civil War veterans, and in early August of that year, Union veterans signed a petition to form a Grand Army

Chouteau County Civil War veterans and ladies. *Overholser Historical Research Center.*

27. Earlier version published in *River Press*, December 19, 2011.

of the Republic post. Signing this list were the following veterans with their rank and regiment:

John J. Donnelly, lieutenant colonel, 14th Michigan Infantry

Mack J. Leaming, major, 6th Tennessee Cavalry/72nd Illinois Infantry

James H. Rice, captain, 27th New York Infantry

William McQueen, regimental quartermaster, 1st Iowa Infantry

Julius L. Stuart, command sergeant, 6th Ohio Infantry

Max Waterman, sergeant, 35th Iowa Infantry

Dan Dutro, musician, 150th Illinois Infantry

William S. Wetzel, corporal, 25th Iowa Infantry

George W. Crane, corporal, 26th Illinois Infantry

Thomas A. Cummings, Battery C, 1st New York Light Artillery

Edward W. Lewis, private, 113th Illinois Infantry

George M. Bell, private, 13th Maine Infantry

Thomas Coatsworth, private, 46th Wisconsin Infantry

Frank Coombs, private, 129th Indiana Infantry

James Werrick, private, 129th Indiana Infantry

Robert S. Culbertson, private, 6th Ohio Infantry

The Fort Benton post was approved by the Montana Department GAR and designated the G.K. Warren Post No. 20, GAR, Fort Benton. The name honored Brigadier General G.K. Warren, a hero at Little Round Top during the Battle of Gettysburg. At a critical point in the battle, Union general George Meade sent his chief engineer, Brigadier General Gouverneur K. Warren, to find a way to block the advance of Confederate soldiers on the flank of Union forces. Climbing Little Round Top, Warren found only a small signal corps station there. He saw the glint of bayonets in the sun to the southwest and realized that a Confederate assault into the Union flank was imminent. He hurriedly sent officers to find help from any available units in the vicinity. Colonel Strong Vincent, commander of the Third Brigade, seized the initiative and directed his four regiments to Little Round Top. Upon arrival, Vincent received fire from Confederate batteries almost immediately. On the western slope, he placed the 16th Michigan, and then proceeding counterclockwise were the 44th New York, the 83rd Pennsylvania and, finally, at the end of the line on the southern slope, the 20th Maine.

Arriving only ten minutes before the Confederates, Vincent ordered his brigade to take cover and wait and ordered Colonel Joshua Lawrence Chamberlain, commander of the 20th Maine, to hold his position, the extreme left flank of the Army of the Potomac, at all costs. Chamberlain and his 385 men waited for what was to come. For their heroic actions,

Grand Army of the Republic and United Confederate Veterans marching at the Gettysburg 1913 Encampment. *Library of Congress.*

Chamberlain received the Medal of Honor. The citation read that the medal was awarded for "daring heroism and great tenacity in holding his position on the Little Round Top against repeated assaults, and carrying the advance position on the Great Round Top." The 1974 novel *The Killer Angels* and its 1993 film adaptation, *Gettysburg*, depicted a portion of the important Battle of Little Round Top.

HELENA'S CONFEDERATE MONUMENT HONORING THE NOSTALGIC LOST CAUSE PAST[28]

For those who believe Montana was far removed from the Civil War, take a stroll through Helena's Hill Park and admire the granite fountain prominently standing there. You are viewing the Confederate Memorial Fountain erected by the Daughters of the Confederacy in 1916. As you read the inscription,

28. Earlier version published in *Tribune,* July 29, 2012.

Helena's Confederate Memorial, northernmost monument to the Confederacy in the United States. *Author's photo.*

"A Longing Tribute to Our Confederate Soldiers," realize that you are in the presence of the oldest Confederate monument in the Northwest and one of the few such tributes to the Confederacy in the northern United States.

Hill Park is located south of the distinctive mosque-like Civic Center between Neill Avenue and North Park Avenue. This location is near the heart of the capital city on the western rim of historic Last Chance Gulch.

Confederate Veteran magazine of January 1, 1917, reported the unveiling of this Confederate memorial:

> *The 5th of September, 1916, was made memorable in the city of Helena, Mont., by the presentation of the Confederate memorial fountain as a gift from the Winnie Davis Chapter, U.D.C. It was in 1903 that this Chapter began its work for a Confederate memorial, and in this it was aided by other Chapters of the State. So on the evening of September 5, in the glow of the low Montana twilight, an interested throng gathered to witness the unveiling ceremonies.*

Several aged Confederate veterans were present in places of honor. Miss Gertrude C. Young gave the presentation speech, telling the history of the gift as the Confederate Daughters saw the need to beautify Hill Park. She explained the motive in planning such a gift, telling how the Confederate Daughters, desiring to make some presentation to their new residence after leaving the South, had decided on the fountain as a fitting memorial. Miss Young lauded the present-day American spirit, a spirit of union with no feeling between the old North and South that caused such bitterness and sorrow years ago. She closed by saying, "On behalf of the daughters of the Confederacy, I present this fountain to the city of Helena as a token of our esteem toward our new home."

City Attorney Edward Horsky, in place of Mayor Purcell, accepted the donation for the city. After the speeches, Mrs. Will Aiken pulled the cord to loosen the flag that covered the monument, while Mrs. F.F. Read turned the water into the bowl. These three ladies were the only charter members of the Winnie Davis Chapter then in Helena.

Prominent Helena architect George H. Carsley, the monument's designer, was inspired somewhat by a memorial fountain erected in Washington, D.C., in the memory of two heroes of the *Titanic* disaster. Erected at a cost of $2,000, the Confederate Memorial used native Montana granite. *Confederate Veteran* described the fountain:

> *The base upon which the fountain is placed is rectangular in form, bordered by heavy granite copings and approaches being on opposite sides, corresponding to the east-and-west axis of the park...On the other sides are granite seats with supports having classic lines. There are two basins. Bubbling drinking fountains at its north and south sides are so designed as to enhance the beauty of the lines of the fountain. The upper basin is about six feet in diameter, supported on an octagonal pedestal springing from the lower basin...*
>
> *Rising out of the upper basin is an octagonal shaft, upon opposite sides of which are two inscriptions in cut letters...Upon one side: "A Longing Tribute to Our Confederate Soldiers." Upon the other... "By the Daughters of the Confederacy in Montana, A.D. 1916."*
>
> *Four bronze spouts spill water from this pedestal into the upper basin. In addition, there are four low jets bubbling through the surface of water in the upper basin, which, together with two overflow spouts from the drinking fountain and the water spilling from the upper into the lower basin, forms pleasing lines and graceful patterns.*
>
> *The whole is surmounted by a bronze lantern, giving to the shaft something of the proportions of a lighthouse, the distance from platform to top of the light being about nine feet.*

To The Departing Confederate Soldiers.

One by one they pass away,
   Cross the river one by one;
And the shadows of to-day
   Darken the departing sun.
'Tis a hero falling, seeking
   In eternity sweet rest,
While his country's tears are reeking
   Sorrow's passion rends the breast
Of the chivalry and beauty
   South of Dixie's magic line.

One by one the ranks are thinning,
   And a comrade falls to sleep.
Death invades our sanctum, winning
   Jewels rare we fain would keep:
Jewels from the Southern cross,
   Tried by fires of deadly war.
Who shall recompense our loss?
   Will their spirits from afar
Whisper us some consolation,
   Minister at freedom's shrine?

by Smith Johnson.
Tyler, Texas.

To the Departed Confederate Soldiers. *United Confederate Veteran Convention, 1895.*
Author's collection.

The Montana Confederate Memorial was dedicated in 1916 at a time when race relations in the country were at the nadir, with segregation and lynchings reaching their peak. The memorial beautified Hill Park, but it also made a strong statement about the past—that even this far north and sixty years after the Civil War, the Confederacy could be honored nostalgically.

WE BEGAN WITH THE QUESTION, "How did the Civil War affect Montana?" As Montana and our nation commemorate the 150th anniversary of the Civil War, the answer emerges from an understanding of the Civil War and the events and people who formed Montana Territory. Our nation lost as many as 750,000 soldier deaths and an unknown number of civilian casualties during the war, none of them in Montana. Yet Montana Territory was forged on battlefields in the East and in the halls of Congress. Streaming to the Montana gold fields were survivors of the war—those who had seen combat and survived, fled the field of battle or chose to avoid service. As the tide turned against the Confederacy in Missouri and Tennessee, many came up the Missouri River or overland to begin new lives. Yankees and Rebels came to the new territory, as did Southern and Northern sympathizers, bringing their families and their strong beliefs with them.

The end of the war brought many more people to the territory, from the North and the South, each with their own scars and memories of the war. For decades to come, the Civil War remained in the minds and hearts of men, women and children, black and white, as they came to frontier Montana. Through veterans' organizations and celebrations of Decoration Day, the war and its casualties were remembered. Homesteaders, land grant college students and descendants of emancipated slaves celebrated the political successes of the war. Today, 150 years and many generations later, our nation and Montana commemorate the Civil War and the profound changes it brought to the lives of us all.

Bibliography

Adams, Paul M. *When Wagon Trails Were Dim.* N.p.: Montana Conference Board of Education, 1957.

Albright, R.E. "The American Civil War as a Factor in Montana Territorial Politics." *Pacific Historical Review* 6 (March 1937): 36–46.

Allen, Frederick. *A Decent Orderly Lynching: The Montana Vigilantes.* Norman: University of Oklahoma Press, 2004.

Ambrose, Stephen E. *Crazy Horse and Custer: The Parallel Lives of Two American Warriors.* New York: Anchor Books, Doubleday, 1975.

Athearn, Robert G. "The Civil War and Montana Gold." Civil War in the West issue. *Montana the Magazine of Western History* 12 (April 1962): 62–73.

———. "West of Appomattox." *Montana the Magazine of Western History* 12 (April 1962): 2–11.

Birney, Hoffman. *Vigilantes.* Philadelphia: Penn Publishing Company, 1929.

Bradley, Lieutenant James H. *The March of the Montana Column: A Prelude to the Custer Disaster.* Norman: University of Oklahoma Press, 1961.

Carley, Kenneth. *Minnesota and the Civil War: An Illustrated History.* St. Paul: Minnesota Historical Society Press, 2000.

Chittenden, Hiram Martin. *History of Early Steamboat Navigation on the Missouri River Life and Adventures of Joseph La Barge, Pioneer Navigator and Indian Trader for Fifty Years Identified with the Commerce of the Missouri Valley.* New York: Francis P. Harper, 1903.

Compiled service records of Confederate soldiers who served in organizations from the state of Missouri.

Confederate Veteran 25 (January 1917): 6–7.

Contributions to the Historical Society of Montana. 10 vols. Helena, MT, 1876–1940.

Creighton, Margaret S. *The Colors of Courage: Gettysburg's Forgotten History: Immigrants, Women, and African Americans in the Civil War's Defining Battle.* New York: Basic Books, 2005.

"Diamond from the Rough": A History of the Fort Benton Methodist Church. N.p., n.d.

Emilio, Luis F. *History of the Fifty-fourth Regiment of the Massachusetts Volunteer Infantry, 1863–65.* Boston: Boston Book Company, 1891.

Fisk, Elizabeth Chester. *Lizzie: The Letters of Elizabeth Chester Fisk, 1864–1893.* Edited by Rex C. Myers. Missoula, MT: Mountain Press Publishing Company, 1989.

Gibbon, Colonel John. *Gibbon on the Sioux Campaign of 1876.* Bellevue, NE: Old Army Press, 1870.

Great Falls Yesterday. WPA, circa 1939.

Hanchett, Leland J., Jr. *Montana's Benton Road.* Wolf Creek, MT: Pine Ridge Publishing, 2002.

Healy, John J. *Life and Death on the Upper Missouri: The Frontier Sketches of Johnny Healy.* Edited by Ken Robison. Charleston, SC: Create Space, 2013.

Hoar, Jay S. *Montana's Last Civil War Veterans.* Temple, ME: Bo-Ink-um Press, 2010.

Hopewell, M. *Camp Jackson: History of the Missouri Volunteer Militia of St. Louis.* St. Louis, MO: George Knapp & Co. Printer, 1861.

Howard, Joseph Kinsey. *Montana High, Wide, and Handsome.* New illustrated ed. New Haven, CT: Yale University Press, 1959.

———. *Strange Empire: A Narrative of the Northwest.* New York: William Morrow and Co., 1952.

Intermountain and Colorado Catholic, January 2, 1909.

James, Jon G. "Lt. James H. Bradley: The Literary Legacy of Montana's Frontier Soldier-Historian." *Montana the Magazine of Western History* 59 (Winter 2009): 46–57.

Kirkman, Paul. *The Battle of Westport: Missouri's Great Confederate Raid.* Charleston, SC: The History Press, 2011.

Koury, Michael J. *Military Posts of Montana.* Bellevue, NE: Old Army Press, 1970.

Langford, Nathaniel P. *Vigilante Days and Ways.* Missoula: Montana University Press, 1957.

Leeson, Michael A. *History of Montana, 1739–1885.* Chicago: Warner, Beers & Co., 1885.

Lind, Robert W. *Brother Van: Montana Pioneer Circuit Rider.* N.p., 1992.

Loewen, James W. *Lies Across America: What Our Historic Sites Get Wrong.* New York: Touchstone, 2000.

Lytle, Harry W. (pictures by) and verses by Ed H. Cooney. *Well Known Great Falls Men Cartooned.* N.p., 1913.

Maginnis, Martin. "At Gettysburg: The First Minnesota." *Gettysburg Star & Sentinel,* June 14, 1882.

Manion, John S. *General Terry's Last Statement to Custer.* El Segundo, CA: Upton & Sons, Publishers, 2000.

McConnell, Stuart. *Glorious Contentment: The Grand Army of the Republic, 1865–1900.* Chapel Hill: University of North Carolina Press, 1992.

McManus, John C. *American Courage, American Carnage: 7th Infantry Chronicles.* New York: Tom Doherty Associates, 2009.

McPherson, James M. *War on the Waters The Union and Confederate Navies, 1861–1865.* Chapel Hill: University of North Carolina Press, 2012.

Miller, Don, and Stan B. Cohen. *Military & Trading Posts of Montana.* Missoula, MT: Pictorial Histories Publishing Company, 1978.

Mills, Edward Laird. *Plains, Peaks and Pioneers: Eighty Years of Methodism in Montana.* Portland, OR: Binfords & Mort, 1947.

Missouri Digital Heritage Collection. Lieutenant Colonel Malone Letter to Senator James H. Lane, November 28,1864.

Montana Cowboy Hall of Fame. www.montanacowboyfame.com/151001/326007.html.

Montana Digital Newspaper Project.

Montana Historical Society Research Center Vertical Files.

Montana Newspaper Association: *Big Timber Pioneer,* January 26, 1920; *Dillon Examiner,* January 19, 1921; *Gentana Reporter,* November 12, 1917; *Mountaineer,* July 18, 1927; *Whitefish Pilot,* November 27, 1926.

Morris, Robert C. *Readin, 'Riting, and Reconstruction: The Education of Freedmen in the South 1861–1870.* Chicago: University of Chicago Press, 1981.

Muller, William G. *The Twenty-fourth Infantry Past and Present.* Fort Collins, CO: Old Army Press, 1972.

Nankivell, John H., comp. and ed. *The History of the Twenty-fifth Regiment United States Infantry 1869–1926.* Fort Collins, CO: Old Army Press, 1972.

Newspapers: *Billings Gazette, Cascade Courier, Fort Benton Record, Fort Benton River Press, Great Falls Leader, Great Falls Tribune, Helena Herald, Helena Independent Record, Missouri Democrat, Missouri Republican, Montana Post, Rocky Mountain Gazette, St. Louis Globe-Democrat.*

Nolan, Alan T. *The Iron Brigade: A Military History.* Bloomington: Indiana University Press, 1994.

Nolan, Alan T., and Sharon Eggleston Vipond, eds. *Giants in Their Black Hats: Essays on the Iron Brigade.* Bloomington: University of Indiana Press, 1998.

Oates, Stephen B. *A Woman of Valor: Clara Barton and the Civil War.* New York: Free Press, 1995.

Online resources: Ancestry.com; Army and Navy Civil War Service, Enlistment, and Pension Records; Fold3 Civil War Compiled Records; Wikipedia.

Overholser Historical Research Center [OHRC] Vertical Files. Fort Benton, MT.

Overholser, Joel F. *Fort Benton World's Innermost Port.* N.p., 1987.

Ovitt, Mable. *Golden Treasure.* Caldwell, ID: Caxton Printers, 1952.

"Partial Sketch of the Civil and Military Service of Major Martin Maginnis." *Contributions to the Historical Society of Montana* 8 (1917): 7–24.

Philpott, William Bledsoe, ed. *The Sponsor Souvenir Album and History of the United Confederate Veterans' Reunion, 1895.* Houston, TX, 1895.

Pollard, Edward A. *The Lost Cause: A New Southern History of the War of the Confederates.* New York: E.B. Treat & Co., Publishers, 1866.

Progressive Men of Montana. Chicago: A.W. Bowen & Co., circa 1903.

Purple, Edwin Ruthven. *Perilous Passage: A Narrative of the Montana Gold Rush, 1862–63.* Edited by Kenneth N. Owens. Helena: Montana Historical Society Press, 1995.

Rable, George C. *Civil War: Women and the Crisis of Southern Nationalism.* Urbana: University of Illinois Press, 1989.

Rademacher, Verle. "Joseph W. Meeks." In *Mountains of Gold, Hills of Grass: A History of Meagher County,* edited by Joan Rostad. Martinsdale, MT: Bozeman Fork Publishing, 1994.

Reese, Timothy J. *Sykes' Regular Infantry Division, 1861–1864: A History of Regular United States Infantry Operations in the Civil War's Eastern Theater.* Jefferson, NC: McFarland & Company, Inc., 1990.

Robinson, John Marion. Family Papers. Montana State University, Merrill G. Burlingame Special Collection 12.

Rockwell, Ronald V. *The U.S. Army in Frontier Montana.* Helena, MT: Sweetgrassbooks, 2009.

Rowe, Mrs. Clarence J. (Conrad), comp. *Mountains and Meadows: A Pioneer History of Cascade, Chestnut Valley, Hardy, St. Peter's Mission, and Castner Falls 1805 to 1925.* N.p., n.d.

Sanders, Helen Fitzgerald. *A History of Montana.* 3 vols. Chicago: Lewis Publishing Company, 1913.

Sanders, Wilbur F. "Address of Hon. Wilbur F. Sanders, at the Dedication of the Capitol of Montana, the Pioneers." Historical Society of Montana, Contributions, vol. 1 (Helena, 1903), 122–23, 137.

Shaw, Robert Gould. *"Blue-Eyed" Child of Fortune: The Civil War Letters of Colonel Robert Gould Shaw.* Edited by Russell Duncan. Athens: University of Georgia Press, 1992.

Small, Lawrence F., ed. *Religion in Montana: Pathways to the Present.* 2 vols. N.p., 1995.

Smurr, J.W. "Jim Crow Out West." In *Historical Essays on Montana and the Northwest.* Helena, MT, 1957, 149–203.

Spence, Clark C. "Spoilsman in Montana." *Montana the Magazine of Western History* 18 (April 1968).

———. *Territorial Politics and Government in Montana 1864–1889.* Urbana: University of Illinois Press, 1976.

Thrapp, Dan L. *Encyclopedia of Frontier Biography.* 4 vols. Lincoln: University of Nebraska Press, 1988–94.

U.S. Census Bureau. Eleventh Census of the United States 1890 Schedules Enumerating Union Veterans and Widows of Union Veterans and Widows of Union Veterans of the Civil War. Montana Bundle 96. Microfilm, National Archives, Washington, D.C., 1948.

———. Various U.S. Census and Slave Schedules.

Walberg, Donna. *So Be It: A History of the Barker Mining District Hughes and Barker.* N.p., 1989.

Waldron, Ellis. *An Atlas of Montana Politics Since 1864.* Missoula: Montana State University Press, 1958.

West, Roberta B. *Brother Van: By Those Who Knew Him.* Monarch, MT: Little Belt Press, 1975.

White, Helen McCann, ed. *Ho! For the Gold Fields: Northern Overland Wagon Trains of the 1860s.* St. Paul: Minnesota Historical Society, 1966.

Wylie, Paul R. *The Irish General Thomas Francis Meagher.* Norman: University of Oklahoma Press, 2007.

Index

About the Author

K en Robison is an author and historian who lives in Great Falls, Montana, with his wife, Michele. Ken, a native Montanan, is historian at the Overholser Historical Research Center in Fort Benton. He serves as historian for the Great Falls/Cascade County Historic Preservation Commission and is active in historic preservation throughout Montana. Ken writes monthly columns on Montana's Civil War veterans for two newspapers. His books include *Life and Death on the Upper Missouri: The Frontier Sketches of Johnny Healy*; *Cascade County and Great Falls*; and *Fort Benton*. He writes historical articles for *Montana the Magazine of Western History* and other regional journals. He is a retired navy captain after a career in naval intelligence. The Montana Historical Society honored Ken as "Montana Heritage Keeper" in 2010.

Visit us at
www.historypress.net
....
This title is also available as an e-book